Oliver Dyer

Great senators of the United States forty years ago

1848 and 1849

Oliver Dyer

Great senators of the United States forty years ago
1848 and 1849

ISBN/EAN: 9783337153106

Printed in Europe, USA, Canada, Australia, Japan

Cover: Foto ©Suzi / pixelio.de

More available books at **www.hansebooks.com**

GREAT SENATORS

OF THE

UNITED STATES FORTY YEARS AGO,

(1848 AND 1849.)

WITH

PERSONAL RECOLLECTIONS AND DELINEATIONS

OF

CALHOUN, BENTON, CLAY, WEBSTER, GENERAL HOUSTON, JEFFERSON DAVIS,

AND OTHER

DISTINGUISHED STATESMEN OF THAT PERIOD.

BY

OLIVER DYER.

NEW YORK:
ROBERT BONNER'S SONS,
Publishers.

PRESS OF
THE NEW YORK LEDGER.
NEW YORK.

THE AUTHOR'S PREFACE,

——— ‒

My main purpose in writing this book was to tell some interesting things (which I suppose nobody else can tell) about distinguished statesmen who came under my personal observation when I was a reporter in the United States Senate, more than forty years ago, and of whose characters I have made particular study.

For the benefit of persons who are not familiar with the public affairs and public men of the past, I have found it expedient, in telling those things which are only within my own personal knowledge, to relate other things which are within the information of every student of our history ; and the well-informed critic may think that in some cases I have been too particular in relating what is so familiar to

him, he supposes everybody must be acquainted
with it.   But I have had experiences in lectur-
ing during the last twenty years on the subjects
discussed in this book, which teach me that in
writing for the people at large, one cannot be
too particular or too plain, nor too repetitive as
to names and dates. As an indication of the
correctness of my views on this point, I will
mention that a few years ago I lectured on Calhoun, Benton, Clay and Webster in a neighboring
city, and the next day, one of the reporters who
were present, informed the readers of the paper
by which he was employed that "Calhoun was
a forgotten member of Congress from Missouri,"
and that "Benton was a half-civilized old
buffer from the hill country of North Carolina."
   Wherever I have lectured on the subjects set
forth in this volume it has occasioned surprise
that I (an abolitionist so long as slavery existed,
and a Republican who quadriennially put on
the bloody-shirt as long as that ensanguined
underwear was in political vogue) should
speak so kindly, and in some respects eulogisti-
cally, of John C. Calhoun and Jefferson Davis.
As to that, I will only say that I spoke of those

gentlemen in my lectures, and have written of them in this book, as I found them ; and it is pleasant to remember that wherever I thus spoke of them in my lectures, my remarks were generously applauded.

In the first chapter of this work I have given a detailed account of the movement by which Henry Clay was defeated and General Taylor nominated in the Whig National Convention of 1848, and of the subsequent political strategy and management which led to Taylor's election ; because the details of the movement are interesting and instructive, and (until now) have never been made known. I supposed and hoped that Thurlow Weed would give a full account of that movement in his autobiography ; he could have written a chapter on it that would have gone blazing down the century ; but, in accordance with his nature and the habits of his life, he repressed his feelings, suppressed his information, and withheld his hand. Ambitious politicians can learn something to their advantage by reading the account of the way in which William H. Seward and Thurlow Weed conducted that campaign ; and veteran statesmen will doubtless follow the movements of those two consummate masters of political strategy with interest, and perhaps with delight.

I have kept the materials for this volume by me, in phonographic short-hand notes, as long as Moses kept sheep for his father-in-law in Midian : forty years. I have always had the intention of some day writing them out for publication ; and now, in the hope that what I have written of the illustrious personages, whose characters I have sought to delineate, may be interesting to their countrymen and useful to other writers, I send forth this little book to the consideration of those who may chance to read it.

OLIVER DYER.

MOUNT VERNON, N. Y.
September, 1889.

TABLE OF CONTENTS.

CHAPTER I.

PRELIMINARY SKETCH OF INTERESTING EVENTS.

I. The Second Session of the Thirtieth Congress, and Political Events Preceding It.—
Session began Dec. 4, 1848. Condition of political
affairs and state of public feeling. Close of the Mexican war. Acquisition of new territory. Shall it
come into the Union as slave or free? Rancorous
bitterness engendered by the question. Fixed policy
of the South on the subject. No new free State without a new slave State. What the abolition wits said
about it. What Col. Benton said about it. Why the
Mexican war was forced on. The Wilmot Proviso.
The unparalleled excitement it occasioned. Discussion of it not ended until Lee surrendered to Grant.
The proviso in the Democratic, and Whig National
Conventions of 1848. Trampled on in the Democratic and smothered in the Whig Convention. Indignation of anti-slavery Democrats and abolition Whigs.
Disloyalty to Henry Clay. My surprise thereat; and

my eyes get opened very wide as to the character and ways of politicians.

II. THE MOVEMENT THAT LED TO THE DEFEAT OF HENRY CLAY.—Manipulated by William H. Seward and Thurlow Weed, of New York, Thomas Butler King, of Georgia, and Truman Smith, of Connecticut. Thurlow Weed chief manager. The motives for the movement. The Whig party in a critical situation. Singular and unexpected effect of the Mexican war upon political parties. General Taylor popular with the Whig rank and file, but not with the leaders. Nomination of General Cass by the Democrats inspires Seward and Weed with hope; why it inspires them with hope. The Free-soil movement. How it must be managed to prevent its defeating the Whig candidate. John P. Hale must be set aside as its leader, and an influential Democrat put in his place. Barnburners and Old Hunkers; their deadly animosity. General Cass; his character; hated by Martin Van Buren; also, the friends of Silas Wright: the hopes his nomination gave to Seward and Weed. A very big "if." How to overcome the big "if."

III. THURLOW WEED; THE SECRET OF HIS POLITICAL POWER.—His pertinacity and sagacity. The Albany *Evening Journal*. The New York press: *Sun*, *Herald*, *Tribune*. The *Times* and *The World* not yet born. Reasons why the Albany *Journal* was then the most influential newspaper in the State of New York. Weed's masterly use of his power. His "personal column." His mode of winning the personal regard of promising young men. Young Frog, of Frog Hol-

my eyes get opened very wide as to the character and
ways of politicians.

CHAPTER II.

GENERAL HOUSTON.—JEFFERSON DAVIS.—JOHN P. HALE.--STEPHEN A. DOUGLAS.—SIMON CAMERON.—HANNIBAL HAMLIN.—ALEXANDER H. STEPHENS.

I. GENERAL SAM HOUSTON.—Thirty States and sixty Senators in 1848. Only two of the Senators now living—Hannibal Hamlin, of Maine, and Jefferson Davis, of Mississippi. Four great Senators—Calhoun, Benton, Clay and Webster—of whom I intend to write particularly. Other Senators worthy of notice. General Houston. The romance which encircled his name. His boyhood. His early popularity. His brilliant career. Elected Governor of Tennessee when thirty-four years old. Marries a beautiful girl. A harrowing discovery. Resigns his governorship and

No news of him attainable. Santa Anna rushing
upon him with an overwhelming force. Inexpressible
public anxiety. The ear of the nation turned to Buena
Vista in an agony of suspense. News at last. A desperate fight and a great victory. A wild revel of public rejoicing. The whole country breaks out into illum-
inations. Glowing accounts of the gallantry and skill of
Colonel Jefferson Davis, of the First Mississippi Volunteers. He holds a vital point against six times his
force. Frightfully wounded and ordered to quit the
field. But he won't go. Has his wound dressed
while sitting in his saddle and holds on. The desperate charge of the Mexican cavalry upon the Mississippians. Colonel Davis forms them into a V. The
Mexicans ride in and are blown from their saddles.
That ends it. Mr. Davis's personal appearance and
bearing. His style and ability as a debater. His
kindness of heart and his courtesy to everybody. He
wins my affection and keeps it, although I was a hot-
hearted young abolitionist and detested his political
principles. My grateful feelings towards him after
forty years.

III. JOHN P. HALE.—The first man elected
United States Senator on a square anti-slavery issue.
Report that his life was threatened. Futile attempt to
browbeat him into silence. What the Methodist Minister from New Hampshire said about Hale. Hale's
courage, his good-nature, his laziness. His wit and
humor. His voice and style of speaking. His readiness at repartee. Senator Foote, of Mississippi, says
they'd hang him if they ever caught him in that State.

CHAPTER III.

JOHN C. CALHOUN.

I. How Calhoun was looked upon in the North.—My own hostile feelings towards him. My first view of him in the Senate. His appearance perfectly satisfactory. He looked like an embodiment of the devil. His personal appearance. The first time I heard him in debate. That everlasting Wilmot Proviso comes up from an unexpected quarter. It brings Calhoun to his feet. He denounces the petition containing the Proviso. His elegant, winning, convincing manner. His charming voice. Benton replies ferociously and exasperatingly. A heated debate. Calhoun maintains his high-toned and captivating manner to its close. My change of feeling towards him. I begin to like him. I don't like my liking him. I think it is traitorous to my abolition principles, but as time goes on I like him better and better, in spite of all I can do.

II. A New Year's call on Calhoun; the State Rights doctrine from his own lips.—I call, at Mr. Calhoun's request, to explain the then new system of phonographic writing to him. His interest in the system and in Master Murphy's exhibitions of rapid writing. He talks about reporting. One mistake which reporters constantly made in reporting his speeches. They represented him as saying " this

CONTENTS. 19

thus following up Quincy's lead. While not attempting to exonerate Calhoun for the consequences of his
political course, I wish to treat the subject fairly and
truthfully. What is sauce for the South Carolina
goose is also sauce for the Massachusetts gander.

IV. CALHOUN'S VIEWS ON THE EDUCATION OF
BOYS AND HIS OPINION OF GENERAL JACKSON.—He
thought Northern people all wrong as to their ideas
and modes of education. Too much cultivation of
the mind and not enough development of body.
South Carolina boys trained differently from Georgia
boys. "Look at that boy!" (Master Murphy.)
How South Carolina boys were trained in Calhoun's
time. What the ultimate result of the northern system of education will be. The people, though intellectually brilliant, will have to take an inferior position in practical affairs. Calhoun probably got a
good deal of satisfaction out of this view of the case.
My question about General Jackson. It was an inex-
cusable blunder. Its effect on Calhoun. His reply.
Its significance ; it seemed to be a vivid revelation of
Calhoun's inward spirit.

CALHOUN'S QUARREL WITH GENERAL JACKSON ;
AND ITS RESULT.—My increasing affection for Calhoun,
and regret at his political course. His splendid career,
from his entry into public life to his rupture with
Jackson. Cause of the rupture. Jackson's high-
handed course in Florida in 1819. His wrath when
Congress censured his course. Threatens to cut off
the ears of Congressmen. President Monroe asks for
the opinion, in writing, of the members of his Cabi-

CHAPTER IV.

THOMAS H. BENTON.

I. BENTON'S HATRED OF CALHOUN.—Benton called the Great Missourian ; Calhoun, the Great South Carolinian. The two men contrasted. Why Benton hated Calhoun.

II. HOW TO ESTIMATE CHARACTER.—The two factors—Heredity and Environment—in the formation of character. Heredity can only be developed, not changed. Tragic incident illustrating this truth. A vegetarian bear. Trying to change a bear from a carnivorous to a herbivorous animal. The tragic result. What are considered unaccountable developments of character explainable by the doctrine · of heredity.

III. BENTON'S CHARACTER.—His heredity. It had characteristics of the bear, the bull and the eagle. Mentally and politically a Roman Senator ; in physique and temper a Roman gladiator. His wonderful body and his wonderful head. His courage and his cunning. His perception, his firmness and

CHAPTER V.

HENRY CLAY.

I. Some of Clay's distinguishing character
istics.—His height. His brilliancy and his chivalry.
His phenomenal popularity and the reason of it. His
rare combination of attractive qualities. His captivating manners. His marvelous memory. His kindness
of heart. His genuine interest in the welfare of his
fellow-citizens. His intense patriotism. The great
champion of American industry. His interest in all
kinds of industrial pursuits and in the people engaged
in them.

II. Leading characteristic of his mind; his
oratory.—Penetration the leading characteristic of
his mind. His great powers of perception. His manner in debate. His wonderful voice. His animation
and vehemence. His speaking countenance. A great
soul on fire. The effect of his oratory enhanced by
the peculiar conformation of his forehead. Sometimes
seemed to be rising in the air and taking the audience
along with him. What an old lady said about the effect of his oratory. The secret of all this. Clay's
unique and unmatchable heredity. His physical
structure. His vital force. His strenuous blood. How
he came to pass, in his totality, and what the net result of it all was. His honesty. "I'd rather be right
than be President." His first solicitude was for his

principles ; his second, for his friends ; his last, for himself. His industry ; his simplicity of life. The people believed in him, and all these things helped his oratory. His "looking countenance." The clearness and simplicity of his style. Clay's speeches are not read now. It is for the same reason that a lover's speeches are not read. They are made for the occasion and not for future ages. Clay spoke to win his cause right there and then and was content with his immediate success. Clay's felicitous style of telling an anecdote. One of his favorite stories.

III. CLAY'S CHIEF FAULT IN DEBATE.—A notable instance of its exhibition. His collision with Calhoun. Their estrangement for years. Their touching reconciliation. A memorable scene. The personal manner of the two great Senatorial veterans contrasted.

IV. THE WAY IN WHICH THE FOUR GREAT SENATORS—CALHOUN, BENTON, CLAY AND WEBSTER—RECEIVED STRANGERS WHO WERE INTRODUCED TO THEM.—The custom of introducing strangers to the "Great Four," by members of Congress. Form of introduction. Calhoun's way of receiving a stranger. Benton's way. His overwhelming and imperious graciousness frightens a stranger. Webster's manner : Cold, ungracious and offensive. He made enemies by it. Clay's manner : affable, captivating and full of tact and good-fellowship. Made friends of the introducers and the persons introduced.

V. TOM MARSHALL'S ANECDOTE.—How the law firm of Breckenridge & Marshall gravitated to the head of the Kentucky bar, with only one exception, and that exception was Henry Clay. How they longed to encounter Clay, so as to put an end to the one exception to their leadership. They watch for an opportunity and find it. How they supposed they had "laid out" Clay forever. But they were mistaken. How the old lion drove Marshall to the bottle and Breckenridge to the Bible with one swoop of his paw.

VI. CLAY'S FELICITY IN EXORDIUM.—A notable example. A sketch leading up to the occasion. His retiracy from the Senate in 1842. His reason for retiring. Treachery of the "Tyler Whigs." Clay's intolerable position. He was missed as soon as he retired. The people wanted him back. Clay's poverty. The old man goes home to Lexington, Kentucky, and resumes the practice of law to earn his daily bread. The spectacle touches the heart of the nation. The rank and file of the Whig party clamor for his nomination for the Presidency in 1844. His enemies alarmed. They set to work to kill him off. A concerted system of defamation. He announces that he will meet his fellow-citizens at Lexington and reply to his defamers. A great multitude assembles to hear him. The composition of the audience. Clay's opening remarks set the people wild. Great excitement. Enemies of Henry Clay looked for, but luckily none were found. His great speech and its great effect. He is nominated for the Presidency by acclamation in '44. A great campaign and a great defeat. A Whig poet's lamentation. The cause of Clay's defeat. His election to the Presidency omitted from the great pro-

CHAPTER VI.

DANIEL WEBSTER.

I. THE GODLIKE DANIEL.—His intellectual superiority over all rivals. His personal appearance; his phenomenal head; his brow; his eyes; his forehead; his majestic personality; his voice; his power of magnifying a word; his hair; his complexion. The overwhelming atmosphere and sense of power which emanated from and surrounded him.

II. HIS FIRST APPEARANCE (OF THE SESSION) IN THE SENATE CHAMBER.—How I knew it was Webster. His reception by the Senate. The attention and respect always paid to him. No other Senator listened to as he was. His miserable health. His appearance and reception whenever he arose to address the Senate; perfect description of him from Paradise Lost.

III. WEBSTER'S MENTAL MAKE-UP.—The most wonderful ever known on the American continent. The operations of his perceptive and reflective faculties. His imagination. His veneration. Some things in which he was unrivalled. What is necessary in order to understand Webster's greatness. Aggregation of inferiority cannot produce superiority. Illustrated by the speed of the famous race-horse Eclipse. His

GREAT SENATORS

OF FORTY YEARS AGO (1848).

———— •••• ————

CHAPTER I.

PRELIMINARY SKETCH OF INTERESTING EVENTS.

I. THE SECOND SESSION OF THE THIRTIETH CONGRESS AND POLITICAL EVENTS PRECEDING IT.

The second session of the Thirtieth Congress began on Monday, December 4th, 1848. I was there as a reporter, in the Senate, for the *National Intelligencer*, which was then a widely circulated and influential newspaper.

The condition of political affairs and the state of public feeling at the beginning of the Congressional session in 1848, excited a good deal of apprehension in the minds of leading statesmen. The Mexican war had but recently closed, and we had acquired a vast stretch of territory, including Arizona, Utah, Colorado, Nevada, New Mexico and California. These Territories were to come into the Union as States; and the question of questions in that day was whether they should come in as slave States or as free States; in other words, whether slavery should be confined within the limits it then occupied or be extended into new territory.

It is impossible to bring the rancorous bitterness which that question then excited within the comprehension of people who were not living and old enough to understand the general course of events at that period.

It was the fixed policy of the South to keep the free States from outnumbering the slave States. By this means, although in a minority in the House of Representatives, they would maintain an equality in the Senate, and thus be enabled to check legislation hostile to slavery. In pursuance of this policy, Florida and Iowa had recently been admitted into the Union at the same time (December, 1846), by the provisions of a bill coupling them together. The abolition wits of the day remarked that things had come to such a pass that a white baby could not now be born into the Union unless a black one was born at the same time. Colonel Benton commented on the contemporaneous admission of the two States in his solemn, sarcastic way, pretending that he was unable to see why two States, one of which was the oldest and the other the newest territory ; one in the extreme north-west of the Union, the other in the extreme south-east ; one the land of evergreens and perpetual flowers, the other the climate of long and rigorous winter, and with nothing whatever either in interest or history, or in fact or in sentiment to unite them, should be cradled in one bill and brought into the Union together.

As there was no more territory out of which slave States could probably be made, the war with Mexico was forced on for the purpose of acquiring territory into which slavery could be extended. The territory had been acquired; and now (1848) here it was, and the contention was whether it should be handed over to slavery or secured to freedom.

In 1846, while the war with Mexico was raging, a bill was introduced into the House of Representatives appropriating two million dollars to defray the expenses of negotiating a peace. The amount of the appropriation was subsequently increased a million dollars, and the measure became known as the three-million bill. While this bill was pending in the House of Representatives, David Wilmot, a Democratic Representative from Pennsylvania, moved to amend it by adding a provision that slavery should not be introduced into any of the territory that should be acquired from Mexico.

That little amendment at once became famous as the Wilmot Proviso. It occasioned a prodigious excitement in Congress, which rapidly spread throughout the country. It greatly embittered and exasperated the South, as well it might, for it struck at the very life of slavery, inasmuch as to limit slavery was to strangle it. Besides, the adoption of such a proviso would defeat the main purpose for which the war with Mexico had been begun and was being carried on. Hence, this fundamental proviso was the reddest rag that could have been waved in the face of the Southern bull, and that brave, belligerent creature responded to the tantalizing provocation with character-istic alacrity and resolution.

After an impassioned and prolonged debate, the proviso was carried in the House of Repre-sentatives (1846), but it was defeated in the Senate. The next year (1847) it was defeated in both Houses of Congress, after a desperate struggle. But although it was killed in Con-gress, it survived in the country. It was acrimoniously discussed and wrangled over in nearly every newspaper, in every school district, at every political meeting and every fireside.

In fact, it may be said that the contest provoked by it was not ended until Robert E. Lee surrendered to Ulysses S. Grant at Appomatox Court House, on April 9th, 1865, nineteen years after David Wilmot offered his little amendment to the three-million bill, in the House of Representatives.

The Wilmot Proviso came up in the national conventions of 1848. In May of that year, the Democratic Convention, at Baltimore, which nominated General Cass for the Presidency, trampled on the Proviso (which was introduced by Preston King, of New York), and thereby offended many of the Northern, Eastern and Western delegates. In the Whig Convention, which met at Philadelphia, in June, a strong effort was made by the anti-slavery section of the party to nominate Henry Clay, who was in favor of the Proviso, although he was a Southerner and a slaveholder. But the friends of Clay were defeated. How and why they were defeated they did not know, and it is probable that the majority of them never knew. I was the official reporter of the Convention, knew several of the delegates intimately, and was frequently in the Committee rooms when the wires were in process of adjustment. A number of the delegates who were drawn into the movement against Clay had rooms at the Butler House, where I was then boarding, and we had repeated talks about the game that was going on. Hence the secret of Clay's defeat, and the means by which it was accomplished, became well known to me.

I vividly remember the astonishment with which I heard the supposed friends of Henry Clay talk about setting him aside because *they* had nothing to gain from his election. "His political affiliations have long been fixed," was the common remark; " he is surrounded by friends of a lifetime, and we young men have nothing to hope from him." I was young, knew but little of politicians, and was so unfamiliar with their ways that I supposed men were nominated for the Presidency and elected to the Presidency on purely patriotic principles, and that the only motive by which public men were actuated was a good, old-fashioned love of country.

It is, perhaps, needless to say that when I emerged from the seething turmoil and trickery of the Convention, my views of public men and their motives had undergone a change. I then for the first time realized the truth of what I had been taught by the Greek historian, that under the instigation of selfishness and the contentions of rivalry, men identify what is advantageous with what is honorable, and what is expedient with what is just, and while simulating sentiments of friendship, maintain an attitude of perfidious antagonism ; that the love of power, originating in avarice and ambition, and the party spirit which is engendered by them when men are fairly embarked in a contest, render the tie of party stronger than the tie of patriotism or of religion ; the seal of good faith being not love of country, or the divine law, but fellowship in schemes of spoliation and self-aggrandisement.

II. The movement that led to the defeat of Henry Clay.

The movement which led to Clay's defeat was manipulated by four men, namely : William H. Seward and Thurlow Weed, of New York ; Thomas Butler King, of Georgia ; and Truman Smith, of Connecticut. There were many others in the game, but those four men did most of the subterranean work ; Thurlow Weed being both engineer and conductor of the underground political railroad. The motives which inspired Mr. Weed grew out of the political situation which, from a Whig stateman's point of view, was exceedingly critical.

It is well known that the annexation of Texas and the Mexican war were brought about by the Democrats, under Southern lead, to strengthen their party by the extension of slavery, and ensure to it a perpetuity of political power. But, singularly enough, the result of the Mexican war had unexpectedly helped to rehabilitate the demoralized Whig party, because both of the great, victorious generals, Scott and Taylor, were Whigs. Both of these generals were talked of as candidates for the Presidency, and both were popular with the people.

Taylor was universally popular as a hero, and a movement in favor of his nomination to the Presidency was started among the people several months before the meeting of the Whig National Convention. This movement did not seem to be favored by the politicians. The Whig party had become largely anti-slavery in the North, and General Taylor was a slaveholder from the far South—from Louisiana, one of the bitterest of the slave States. The situation was so critical, and there was so slight a margin of success, that a majority of the party leaders felt that they could not afford to take any risk whatever. Therefore the betting was in favor of Henry Clay's getting the nomination, until the Democrats nominated General Cass. Then William H. Seward and Thurlow Weed saw their opportunity, if fortune would only favor them.

In order to understand the situation and comprehend why Seward and Weed saw their opportunity in the nomination of General Cass by the Democrats, it must be borne in mind that the Democratic party of the North, as well as the Whig party of that section, had become leavened with anti-slavery sentiments. It must also be remembered that there was a bitter feud in the State of New York between the two sections of the Democratic party—the Barnburners and the Old Hunkers. The Barnburners were largely anti-slavery ; the Old Hunkers were bitterly pro-slavery. Seward and Weed foresaw that in any event there would be a third party in the field in 1848, composed of out and out abolitionists and pronounced " Freesoilers," as the opponents of the extension of

slavery into new territory were called. John
P. Hale, the Free-soil Senator from New
Hampshire, had already been suggested as the
Presidential candidate of this third party—had,
in fact, been nominated the year before (1847)
by a convention held at Cleveland, Ohio.

Seward and Weed knew there was great
danger that, if the third-party movement were
left to shape itself and come into the field with
John P. Hale as its leader, enough Whigs would
be drawn off by it in New England, New York,
Pennsylvania and Ohio to give the election to
the Democrats. They remembered that only
four years before, the Liberty Party defection
in New York, whose vote was cast mainly by
anti-slavery Whigs, had given the Empire State
to Polk and made him President of the United
States. It was as clear as day to the two sagacious Whig leaders that the only chance for the
Whigs to win the Presidential election of 1848
was to give this inevitable third-party movement a Democratic lead, and a Democratic

leader, so as, if possible, to draw off as many Democrats as Whigs from the regular tickets. If that could be done, then New England, New York, Pennsylvania and Ohio would be almost certain to give Whig majorities and render the election of the Whig candidate sure. And now the nomination of General Cass by the Democrats promised to give Seward and Weed their opportunity to turn the third-party movement into a vast Democratic rebellion and bolt.

General Cass was a dull, phlegmatic, lymphatic, lazy man. He had an unusually large brain, but it was so torpid that nothing but a powerful appeal to his selfishness or his vanity could arouse it into action ; and when it was aroused its activity was spasmodic and could not be counted upon for sustained energy. There was not a bit of chivalry in Cass's character, nor an atom of magnetism in his nature. Such a man, of course, could not fail to be destitute of the elements of leadership, and to be incapable of inspiring that personal popular-

ity which counts for so much in great political
contests.

The Democrats nominated Cass as a forlorn
hope, and under an irresistible pressure of circumstances. All through the Mexican war
they had sought to develop a Democratic hero
whose popularity could vie with that of the
victorious Whig generals. But their efforts
had been vain ; no Democratic hero was
evoked ; and the party at last fell back in
mingled despair and hope on General Cass, who
enjoyed a nebulous sort of military fame that
hung dimly on the fast receding horizon of the
war of 1812.

Cass's lack of personal popularity was not
the only weight he had to carry. Although he
did not possess qualities which win enthusiastic
friends, he had those which sometimes make
bitter enemies. Unfortunately for him, in
1844, he confederated with Martin Van Buren's
enemies to prevent " New York's favorite son,"
as Van Buren was called, from getting the

Democratic nomination for the Presidency.
Van Buren and his friends looked upon Cass's
conduct as unpardonably treacherous, and
naturally wished to resent it in an effectual
manner.

Van Buren's strength was greatest in the
States pervaded by the anti-slavery disaffection. The Barnburners of New York were his
partisans almost to a man, and his son John
(Prince John) was their pet orator. If by any
means Martin Van Buren could be induced to
accept the leadership of the third party, the
defeat of Cass and the election of the Whig
candidate would be assured. Thurlow Weed
was all the more confident that this would be
the result, because he had intimate knowledge
of the envenomed exasperation which the
friends of Silas Wright cherished against the
supporters of General Cass. Silas Wright, one
of the ablest men of his time, and one of the
most popular men in the State of New York,
had been a sort of political Siamese twin with

Martin Van Buren, and it was believed by his friends that he had been politically assassinated by the Old Hunkers. His recent death--he died in August, 1847—added intensity to the hatred which his multitude of mourners felt for his alleged political assassins, and if Van Buren could be brought into the field, all this hatred could be turned against Cass.

But Seward and Weed knew if—(and this was a most momentous if)—if Henry Clay should be the Whig candidate for the Presidency, that Van Buren would not come forward as the leader of the third party. Much as he wished for vengeance on Cass, he would not gratify his thirst for it by making Henry Clay, so long the enemy of General Jackson, President of the United States. It was their profound conviction of this fact, and their belief that by proper management Van Buren could be brought to the front, which induced Seward and Weed to enter with all their skill and strength into a plan for defeating Clay and nominating Taylor.

The disaffected Democrats had no ill-feeling towards General Taylor. They had hurrahed over his victories, and helped to celebrate his glory with as much enthusiasm as the Whigs had shown in the same cause. General Taylor had never crossed any politician's path, had never been a political partisan, had, in fact, never voted at a Presidential election. He and General Jackson had been friends; and so Jackson's bosom friend, Van Buren, felt kindly towards him, and would much rather see him than Cass in the Presidential chair. Seward and Weed did not shut their eyes to the fact that the nomination of General Taylor would alienate many anti-slavery Whigs; but they knew that if the coming anti-slavery bolt, which they saw to be inevitable, could be made mainly a Democratic bolt, the loss sustained by the desertion of Whigs would be more than counterbalanced by the accession of Democrats

to the bolters, especially in the State of New
York, by whose vote the election would probably be decided.

III. THURLOW WEED—THE SECRET OF HIS
POLITICAL POWER.

General Cass was nominated at Baltimore,
on Thursday, May 25th. The Whig convention was to assemble at Philadelphia on
Wednesday, June 7th. So there was an inter-
vening fortnight for Thurlow Weed and his
co-adjutors to utilize the nomination of Cass for
the purpose of securing the nomination of Taylor. And here it is expedient to say a few
words about Thurlow Weed, in order that the
secret of his political power may be understood.

Many of Weed's contemporaries believed
him to be unscrupulous ; they all acknowledged
his ability. He was a man of such untiring
industry, and such invincible pertinacity, that
no political trail could be long enough to tire
him out, nor could his almost preternatural

sagacity be thrown off the scent, however intri-
cate the trail might be. And this man con-
trolled the Albany *Evening Journal*, which was
one of the most powerful newspapers then published in the State of New York.

It should be remembered that the events we
are narrating occurred in 1848, before the New
York city press had attained its vast circulation
and predominant influence. At that time, the
New York *Sun*, although it had the largest circulation of any daily paper in the city, was a
comparatively uninfluential journal, chiefly
devoted to advertisements. The *Herald* then
had but a little over 10,000 circulation ; the *Tribune* had less than 8,000 ; not one of the other
daily papers had a circulation of 5,000, and the
Times and the *World* were yet unborn. The
Hudson River railroad was not then built ; the
New York and New Haven railroad was not
then built ; the Erie road was not yet built ;
many other railroads, now in connection with
New York, had not then been projected.

Hence, during all that portion of the year when the navigation of the Hudson River was closed by ice, New York was cut off from communication, except by stage, with the rest of the State.

Albany, from its more central location, thus had a great advantage over New York in its communication with the State at large, especially as there was a continuous line of railroads (since consolidated into the New York Central) running from the capital to Buffalo. And the Albany *Evening Journal* was an older paper than the *Sun*, the *Herald*, or the *Tribune*, it having been established in 1830, the *Sun* in 1833, the *Herald* in 1835, and the *Tribune* in 1841. Besides, the Albany *Evening Journal* was the State organ of the Whig party, and there was probably not a township in the State in which it hadn't a club of subscribers. From these facts it can readily be seen that the *Evening Journal* was a political power in those provincial days. And Thurlow Weed knew how to use this power to the greatest advantage.

Perhaps some of the readers of these pages may remember that column in the Albany *Journal*, in which Weed used to make personal mention of his friends and his foes, in little paragraphs, varying from a line and a-half to a dozen or fifteen lines in length. That column was a prodigious power in the politics of the State of New York. There was seldom a young man, in any part of the State, who gave promise of becoming a person of influence, that was not kindly and flatteringly mentioned in that column, no matter to what party he belonged. And does any one suppose that young men thus mentioned would not feel friendly to Thurlow Weed, and be ready to do him a personal favor?

Let us suppose that young Frog, of Frog Hollow, has been admitted to the bar, and begun to show talents for political leadership. He is a Democrat, and does not patronize the

Albany *Evening Journal*, but takes its Democratic rival, the Albany *Argus*. Some morning
his friends ask him if he has seen the last
number of the Albany *Journal*. He sneeringly
replies that he has not seen it ; that he does not
wish to see it ; that he does not train with that
crowd. His friends tell him that he had better
see it, because it has something about himself
in it. He calls on some Whig who takes the
Journal, obtains a copy of the paper, and reads
a paragraph somewhat like this :

"We learn from friends in Frog Hollow
that there is a young man coming forward in
that part of the State of whom his fellow-citizens have just reason to be proud. We refer to
Augustus Frog, Esq., the rising young lawyer.
We knew Mr. Frog's grandfather when he was
a member of the Legislature more than twenty
years ago, and we had such a high personal
regard for him as to make us regret that he
was on the wrong side in politics."

On reading this paragraph, Augustus Frog,

Esq., the rising young lawyer, feels like playing
a game of leapfrog. He borrows the *Journal*
and rushes off with it to his sweetheart, to his
parents, to his grandfather. The old grandfather's eyes sparkle as he reads the paragraph,
and he says : " Yes, I knew Weed when I was
in the Legislature, and a right good fellow he
was ; and smart, too, now I tell you. I hope
you will go there some day, Augustus, and if
you do, I'll give you a letter of introduction to
Weed. He's the best man in Albany for a
young fellow to know."

In a few years Augustus Frog is elected to
the Assembly on the Democratic ticket. His
grandfather gives him the letter of introduction
to Weed, and on its presentation he is received
with paternal kindness and made to feel as
much at home as though he were in his grandfather's office. It is plain to be seen what the
result of this will be. Mr. Weed's kindness,
shown at a time when the young man feels the

need of a friend, sinks into the depths of his heart and brings forth fruit abundantly.

When one multiplies this young Democratic Frog by scores and by hundreds, and adds all the Whig Frogs that had been hopping through the Legislature for eighteen years, he can form some idea of the number of influential friends that Thurlow Weed had in every part of the State in both of the great political parties. And, of course, Weed had the sagacity to use the tremendous power which this widely extended circle of personal friends gave him, in the most adroit and inoffensive manner. By dropping a few remarks here and a few remarks there in conversation, or by correspondence, in which his real purpose was concealed, he could set the minds of either Whigs or Democrats running in the way he wanted them to go, without exciting the least suspicion that he had any ulterior design in what he said or wrote. Or, if he chose to come out frankly with persons whom he wished to enlist directly in his

schemes, he seldom, if ever, addressed his
appeals for help to inhospitable ears.

During the period which elapsed between
the nomination of General Cass at Baltimore
and the assembling of the Whig National Convention at Philadelphia, Weed was busily
engaged in sympathizing with the enraged
Barnburners, and without seeming to meddle
in their party affairs he helped to inflame their
animosity against Cass to an irrestrainable
degree. Seward was also skillfully at work in
the same missionary line.

IV. WILLIAM H. SEWARD—HOW HE AND WEED
WORKED TOGETHER.

William H. Seward was one of the ablest
and most sagacious men of his time. His
inferior physique' and his incapacity for oratory
prevented the people from perceiving the true
measure of his intellectual greatness. If he
had had the personal presence and the voice
and delivery of Calhoun, Clay or Webster, he

would have rivalled them in oratorical power
and impressed himself upon the minds and the
imaginations of his countrymen as forcibly as
they did. But owing to his physical deficiencies
his great abilities were known only to those
who learned them by studying his writings or
from personal intercourse with him.

In matters of political management in the
State of New York, Seward's sagacity was
unerring and his judgment well nigh infallible.
He knew all the influential men in the State ;
he also knew the local leaders, and cultivated
their friendship. He was particularly gracious
to young men, and easily won their affection
and their confidence. He did not neglect men
of influence, whatever their age ; but he was
more attentive to the young than to the old,
fully realizing that the old are constantly passing off the stage, while the young are perpetually coming on.

Seward had a keen perception of the political
advantage which could be gained by utilizing

religious beliefs and prejudices ; and by the adroit use of a felicitous phrase, embodying a pivotal and aggressive truth, and which could be used as a rhetorical battle cry, he could draw large bodies of religionists and reformers into sympathy with his schemes without letting it be known what his ulterior motives or projects were. In this subtle and far-reaching work Seward was unrivalled. He knew just when the fruit was ripe for his hand to pluck. No eagle ever poised over its prey with keener eye, or swooped upon its quarry with surer stroke. In these respects his sagacity and executive spontaneity approached the superhuman. It is doubtful if there ever was a man who had more aptitude than Seward possessed for saying just exactly the right thing in just exactly the right way at just exactly the right time and under just exactly the right circumstances.

Seward's social qualities were a source of strength to him. He was attached to his friends and stood by them, and they were attached to

and stood by him in return. He was eloquent
and masterful in conversation and in intimate
confidential correspondence, and could probably
do more work in twenty-four hours and keep at
his work more continuously than any other man
of his day, except Horace Greeley. Such capac-
ity for work as he had, when directed by such
sagacity as he possessed, is apt to make its way
against any degree of talent or genius which is
unsupported by plodding industry and assid-
uous application.

Seward and Weed understood each other
intimately, and worked together in perfect
accord. What two such men could accomplish
in a field which furnished them with lines of
operation exactly fitted to their powers, and
surrounded by circumstances in which they
both delighted to put their powers forth, cannot be told; and it would be rash to limit
their achievements by ordinary standards of
measurement. In the political contest of 1848,
they knew just exactly what they must accom-

plish in order to win, and they pursued their
course with clear vision, fixed purpose and
unfaltering steps. They subtly and successfully drew their lines through and around the
disaffected political elements in the State, and
especially in the City of New York. They had
the hearty co-operation of several of the leading
Barnburners, who were so determined to wreak
vengeance on General Cass and the Old Hunkers that they gladly availed themselves of any
means which promised to gratify their desires.

It was arranged to hold a public meeting of
Barnburners, in the City Hall Park, to express
their indignation at the manner in which their
delegates had been treated at the Baltimore
Convention. The day on which this meeting
should be held was of great importance to
Seward and Weed, and with the aid of their
Barnburner friends that matter was easily
arranged. The meeting was called for the
afternoon of June 6th, the day before the Whig
Convention was to assemble in Philadelphia.

On the forenoon of that day there was a meeting at the Astor House of Whig delegates from New England, New York, and the Western States. This meeting had been brought about in a seemingly accidental way by Weed. He had been in correspondence with such delegates as he thought it prudent to manipulate, and suggested to them individually that if they would stop over a day in New York, on their way to Philadelphia, "it would be advantageous to the interests of the party." Weed's correspondents told their colleagues that they were going to stop over a day in New York ; the colleagues, of course, wanted to stop over with them : and the result was that the Astor House meeting was largely attended. But little was done at this meeting, its object being, as Weed said, "to have a friendly interchange of views, with an eye to promoting harmony in the convention and securing the ultimate success of the party." But for unsuspecting delegates to "interchange views" with Thurlow Weed, on such an occasion, was pretty sure to end in a change of views on the part of the unsuspecting delegates.

The chief object in having the delegates stop over in New York on that day, was that they might witness the Barnburner meeting in the afternoon. That meeting was one of the largest and most enthusiastic that had ever been held in the city. The names of the committee of Barnburner delegates to the Baltimore convention, who made the delegates' report to the meeting, will be read with interest. They were names which, in those days, were always received with hurrahs in Democratic meetings. They were Churchill C. Cambreling, John A. Kennedy, Robert H. Maclay, William F. Havemeyer and Samuel J. Tilden. The report of the committee was outspoken and inflammatory. It told the vast multitude of exasperated Barnburners that their delegates to the Baltimore convention had been insulted and disfranchised, and it called upon the people to rebuke the per-

with the crowds, took note of what was occur-
ring, and were of course unspeakably anxious to
turn all this Democratic disaffection to the
advantage of the Whig party ; and William H.
Seward and Thurlow Weed devoted themselves
to showing the delegates how their wishes could
be gratified.

They delicately felt the opinions of the delegates and caressed their way into their private
predilections and personal prejudices.　They
found that the preference for Clay was in the
ascendant, that General Scott was the second
choice of many delegates, and that Webster was
the favorite of the New Englanders.　There did
not seem to be any enthusiasm for General
Taylor.　Ohio was strenuously opposed to him,
and nearly solid for Scott.　New England's first
choice was Webster, and her second was Clay.
New York was for Clay, with a leaning to
Scott.　Things looked unequivocally ominous
for the Taylor movement.　Seward and Weed
took, and instructed their lieutenants to take a

gloomy view of the Whig cause. The anticipated Free-soil bolt, with John P. Hale at its
head, was magnified into a political bugaboo.
Hale must be headed off, or the Whigs were
doomed. If the Barnburners could only be
pushed on to take the lead in the Free-soil bolt
and nominate an influential Democrat—perhaps
Martin Van Buren—for their candidate, the
situation would be radically changed, and the
success of the Whig nominee would be rendered
almost sure. But the course of the Barnburners
would be largely influenced by the proceedings
of the Whig Convention. If it should put forward a candidate who was obnoxious to Van
Buren and his friends, they would not help
elect him by bolting. On the other hand, if the
Whigs should nominate a candidate who would
not be personally objectionable to Van Buren and
his friends, the probability was that the Barnburners would organize an independent movement, with Van Buren for their leader. Should
they do this, the Empire State would certainly

be carried by the Whigs, and that would doubtless give them a majority of the electoral votes,
and ensure the election of the Whig candidate.
With such ideas were the minds of the Whig
delegates inseminated.

V. The Whig National Convention of 1848. How Clay was defeated and Taylor nominated.

The next morning (June 7th) in Philadelphia, it was found that Pennsylvania's first
choice was Clay, and her second Taylor; also,
that Taylor was strong in the South and South-
west. It was evident that Clay's popularity
was so great that, if the managers of his canvass evinced a high degree of skill, it would be
very difficult, if not impossible, to defeat him.
But Clay was unfortunate in his friends. They
were enthusiastic and boastful, and felt so sure
of success that they neglected the means of
securing it. On the other hand, the leaders of
the Taylor movement worked with strenuous

energy and surpassing skill. Truman Smith took charge of the New England delegations. Thomas Butler King, assisted by a large number of trusty assistants, worked among the delegates from the South. Pennsylvania and Ohio were left in the hands of influential citizens of their own, who best knew how to work upon their delegates. Weed took especial charge of the New York delegation. In fact, every delegation was skillfully handled. As Ohio could not be brought into line for Taylor, her delegates were encouraged to stand by General Scott, under the belief that the Convention would finally fall back on him as a compromise candidate. Delegates from New York and other States, who felt that they were committed against Taylor, were induced to vote for Scott. New England men, who could not be won over to Taylor, were encouraged to stand by Webster to the last. The younger delegates from all quarters of the Union were indoctrinated with the idea (heretofore mentioned) that if

Clay should be elected President, *they* could not hope for political preferment, as he would bestow all his patronage upon his old friends with whom he had been affiliated for scores of years. The only way for *them* to gain anything by the triumph of the Whig party was to elect a President who had no fixed relations with anybody, so that everyone would have an equal chance. In this way, Clay's strength was insidiously undermined, while his friends were singing Clay songs and hurrahing over his anticipated triumph. Exhilarated by their own enthusiasm, they saw everything in the illusive light of unreflecting hope ; inflated with arrogant confidence, they fatuously derided the monitions of prudence, and peremptorily rebuffed incitations to vigilance.

The Convention was organized on Wednesday, June 7th. John M. Morehead, of North Carolina, was elected permanent President of the Convention. This was thought to be a triumph for Clay, and made his friends feel still

more sure of his nomination. The first day
of the Convention was devoted to preliminary
and routine work, but it was understood that
the balloting for a candidate would be called on
early on Thursday morning. It was arranged
that in balloting, the roll of members should be
called by States in their alphabetical order ; the
name of the chairman of a State delegation to
be called first, and the names of his colleagues
to follow in alphabetical order. On the surface,
this appeared to be a matter of insignificant
detail ; but when it is remembered that, as there
was then no State of California or Colorado,
Connecticut would come third on the list, and
be the first Northern State called, and that
Truman Smith was chairman of the Connecticut delegation, the intelligent reader may be
able to see that the manner of calling the roll
was by no means an insignificant matter.

When the Convention assembled on Thursday morning, in the great hall of the old
Chinese Museum, the friends of Clay hurried on

the balloting, feeling sure that their favorite would lead the poll, and the most sanguine of them offered to bet that he would be nominated on the first ballot. But as the voting went on, a great silence fell on the vast concourse. Delegates who had been counted on for Clay, voted for Taylor, and others voted for Scott. The wily Truman Smith voted for Clay, and so did his five colleagues. The time had not come for him to show his hand. But New England gave Clay only 16 votes, while she gave Webster 21 and Taylor 6. New York gave Webster 1, John M. Clayton 1, Scott 5, and Clay 29. Pennsylvania gave Clay 12, Taylor 8, Scott 6. All this was a surprise to the friends of Clay, but Ohio fairly stunned them. She gave Clay but one vote. She also gave Taylor 1, and Judge McLean 1, and all the rest—20 of them—were given to Scott. As these developments went on, cries of " Treach- ery !" were heard in different parts of the hall, and the Clay men hissed some of the more prominent of the alleged traitors. Almost everybody had kept tally, but the official announcement of the vote was awaited with breathless eagerness. "Amid a silence that could be heard," as Haskell, of Tennessee, said, the secretary read the result : Webster 22, Scott 43, Clay 97, Taylor 111. Another ballot was called for, and after much delay it was taken. The Clay men had labored with their deserters, and hoped for a better result on the second ballot. But they were doomed to disappointment ; when the vote was announced it was found that Webster had held his 22 votes, that Scott had gone up from 43 to 49, that Taylor had gone from 111 to 118, and that Clay had sunk from 97 to 86. Truman Smith and his five colleagues had again voted for Clay, and the staunchness of the Connecticut delegation gave a basis for hope to Clay's friends, who now moved an adjournment, lest Taylor should be nominated on a third ballot. The friends of Webster, and the Ohio delegation supported the motion to adjourn, and it was carried, amid great excitement.

During the interval, between the adjournment of the Convention and its reässembling the next morning, the friends of Clay exhibited lamentable lack of tact and judgment. Instead of trying to win back the deserters by proper appeals and arguments, they vehemently assailed them, and wounded their self-love by vituperative denunciation. Taylor's friends, on the other hand, talked only of the controlling interests of the Whig party and the welfare of the country. They didn't care particularly for any particular individual. All they wanted was a candidate with whom they could win, and thus benefit the country at large while promoting the welfare of the party. At any rate, every delegate had a right to his own opinion, and to vote for whomsoever he believed to be the best man to bear the Whig standard in the coming close and desperate fight. What they admired in a delegate, above all other qualities, was independence of thought and manliness in action.

Such talk was deliciously soothing to the delegates whom Clay's friends were anathematising, and kept them securely in line for Taylor, for whom they would either vote directly, or help indirectly by voting for Webster or Scott. It did more ; it made them partisans against Clay, and set some of them at work to bring their colleagues into coälescence with themselves.

When the Convention met on Friday morning the feeling of apprehension and expectation was so intense that men spoke in hushed voices and walked on tiptoe. As soon as the preliminary routine could be got through with, a motion was made that the Convention proceed to a third ballot for a candidate for the Presidency. The motion was carried by a unanimous vote, but the "aye" was given in such suppressed tones that its effect was like that of the pianissimo of a grand orchestra. The roll call began and proceeded through the lists of delegates from Alabama and Arkansas in deep silence. Next came Connecticut, which, under the lead of Truman Smith, had voted solid for Clay on the two previous ballots. Rumors had circulated during the morning that Smith had gone over to Taylor, and now, when his name was about to be called, the excitement, though subdued, was intense. Smith's smooth-shaven, pink and white face rises before me as I write, and it seems as though I could hear his voice as I heard it forty-one years ago, when, in answer to the call of his name, he responded in clear, penetrating tones : " Zachary Taylor." That vote sounded the knell of Henry Clay. The Taylor men had all got ready for this signal, and when it was given, they burst out with repeated cheers and nearly stampeded the Convention.

When the result of the ballot was announced, and it was known that General Taylor had received 133 votes and Henry Clay only 74, a scene of the stormiest confusion ensued. Some of the delegates cheered till they were exhausted. Others leaped upon seats and chairs and yelled themselves hoarse in trying to get a hearing. Horace Greeley, who was wild for Clay, and General James Watson Webb, who was equally wild for Taylor, ran back and forth between the reporters' table and the platform, shouting and gesticulating like madmen : Webb, with his hat on the back of his head and his coat-tails flapping in the breeze which he occasioned, and Greeley with the knot of his necktie under his left ear and the ends floating over his shoulder. Every one foresaw the result of the next ballot, and when it was taken, and General Taylor was declared nominated—(he getting 171 votes, and Clay only 32, while Scott's had run up to 63) the excitement was not increased, but had somewhat diminished.

As soon as the confusion had subsided, delegates all through the hall began to vocifer-

ate charges of treachery. The Ohio delegation
was exceedingly bitter and exasperated. It
had given Taylor and Clay only one vote a-
piece, and after the first ballot had plumped 21
votes for Scott, every time, under the lure that
he was the "dark horse" of the convention,
who would eventually win the race. But now
they saw that they had been hoodwinked, and
were furious at the discovery. Several of them
made violent speeches, and swore, with uplifted
hand, that, so help them God, they would go
home and do all they could to defeat the nomination. Delegates from Maine, New Hampshire and Massachusetts did likewise. At first,
these demonstrations were received by the
victors with derisive laughter. But after a
while it became apparent that the disaffection
was no laughing matter. Pennsylvania and
New York delegates began to join in the clamors
of indignation. The Taylor men became
alarmed and sought to placate their irate

opponents. But their efforts at pacification were futile.

In the midst of the turmoil a motion was made to proceed to the nomination of a candidate for the Vice-Presidency. The motion was declared carried, and delegates were requested to name their candidates. This brought the Convention to order. Hurried consultations were held by the Taylor men, who hoped to conciliate the disaffected delegates by giving them a candidate for Vice-President who should be a man after their own hearts. It had been arranged that Abbot Lawrence, of Massachusetts, should be the candidate for Vice President, and it was understood that if he got the nomination he would contribute one hundred thousand dollars to the campaign fund. But the impassioned indignation of the anti-slavery portion of the Convention at the nomination of Taylor, so alarmed the general's supporters, that they did not dare to carry out that arrangement. It was seen that something

very decided must be done to pacificate the
anti-slavery disaffection, or there would be a
fatal bolt. Abbot Lawrence was not enough of
an abolitionist to satisfy the disaffected ones.
Who would satisfy. them? was now the question. Of all the names mentioned for the Vice-
Presidency, that of Millard Fillmore, who was
an anti-slavery man of pronounced type, had
most promise in it. Just at the right moment,
Mr. Morril, one of Fillmore's friends from
western New York, leaped upon a bench and
cried: "Give us Millard Fillmore, and we
promise you the vote of New York!"

This declaration was received with cheers,
and Fillmore was nominated. And so a ticket
was provided which it was supposed could walk
over the country from East to West, with its
pro-slavery foot in the South and its anti-slavery
foot in the North, without danger that either
foot would get mired. But the Convention
adjourned amidst an atmosphere of despondency
and gloom. The bitterness of the Clay men

was so intense that they threatened the ticket with defeat and the hopes of the Whig party with annihilation. A premonition of coming defeat seemed to weigh upon the spirits of the delegates.

In the evening, after the adjournment of the Convention, I was in the office of the Philadelphia *North American*, writing out my report. The Hon. Morton McMichael, the editor of the *North American* (who was a gentleman of much social influence and great political sagacity), was talking over the situation with several delegates (Taylor men) from the South west, when who should come tramping into the office, carpet bag in hand, but Horace Greeley. On seeing who were present, Greeley scowled upon them, turned around, and started for the door.

"Where are you going, Mr. Greeley?" McMichael courteously asked.

"I'm going home," snarled Greeley.

"But there's no train to-night," McMichael suggested.

"I don't want any train," Greeley snapped out ; "I'm going across New Jersey, afoot and alone !" And away he went.

As I withdrew my gaze from Greeley's retreating form, it fell upon a dark young man of small stature, with a large and fine head, who was standing at the foot of the table at which I sat. He had been watching Greeley, and his countenance was convulsed with scorn and detestation, somewhat relieved by a sinister gleam of triumph. He soon left the office, and I said to McMichael, "How that man hates Greeley ! Who is he?"

"I thought you knew him," McMichael answered. "He is a fellow-townsman of yours. He is Henry J. Raymond, the *reasoning* editor of the New York *Courier and Enquirer*. Greeley will never forgive him and Colonel Webb for the part they played in the defeat of Clay."

Greeley did not forgive them ; and there were many things for which they didn't forgive

Greeley ; and the personal animosities of those three eminent journalists helped to kill the Whig party, which gave its last national gasp four years afterwards, in 1852.

On the evening of the day after the adjournment of the Convention, the Whigs of Philadelphia, who were nearly all idolatrous worshipers of Clay, held a "Grand Mass Meeting" at the Musical Fund Hall, to ratify the nominations. I was present to report the proceedings for the *North American.* The meeting was not at all "Grand"; it was the most lugubrious political festivity at which I ever assisted. Hardly anything was heard from the speakers but jeremiads over Clay. The address of Mayor Swift, who presided over the meeting, was almost entirely devoted to expressions of grief on Clay's behalf. He was so overcome by his feelings that he spoke with whimsical incoherency. After a time he put his right foot upon the seat of a chair before him, leaned his elbow upon his knee, dropped his face in his hand, and sobbed aloud. He stood in this position till the audience grew nervous. On recovering somewhat from his emotion, he said—still keeping his attitude, with his face in his hand :

"Permit me, my friends, while bowing to the decrees of fate and the decisions of the Convention, to keep one little corner of my heart green in friendship for him whom I hoped to have for a leader in this campaign—one little green spot on which I can rear a monument to his memory which shall reach to the clouds, and whose summit I can water with my tears as I kneel in sorrow at its base."

"For God's sake, Dyer, take care of the old man's rhetoric !" whispered McMichael, who sat immediately behind me. I suppose the gifted editor did not see how the good old man, while kneeling at the base of a monument that reached the clouds, could at the same time water its summit with his tears.

The character of this "Grand Ratification Meeting" indicates what the state of affairs was

in the Whig city of Philadelphia, where the Convention was held. When the work of the campaign was begun, it soon became evident that
the ticket was not popular anywhere in the
North, East or West. The repugnance of the
anti slavery Whigs to Taylor, could not be
overcome; the indignation of the friends of
Clay could not be appeased. The widespread
disaffection gave great momentum to the Free-
soil movement, which grew so rapidly the Whig
leaders saw that their only hope of success lay
in getting the Barnburners to take the lead of
the movement and bring Van Buren into the
field as its candidate. The Barnburners held a
Convention at Utica and nominated Van Buren,
but he peremptorily declined the honor. His
declination was a severe disappointment to the
Barnburners, and left them all at sea; but it
did not disappoint or discourage Seward and
Weed. They knew Martin Van Buren through
and through, and believed that if the opportunity to avenge himself upon Cass and the South-

ern Democrats were offered to him, under circumstances which he considered worthy of his
own position and dignity, he would embrace it,
beyond all peradventure.

VI. MARTIN VAN BUREN.

Martin Van Buren was a greater and a better
man than his countrymen have ever supposed
him to have been. Superiority was stamped
upon every lineament of his countenance. I
met him and Clay on the same evening, at a
Wistar party (so called after Dr. Wistar), in
Philadelphia, in March, 1848. The opportunity
thus presented for studying, comparing and
contrasting those two men was inexpressibly
gratifying to me. I was a student of phreno-
logy, and I brought all my knowledge of that
subject into play on that occasion. It was the
first time I had seen Van Buren ; Clay I had
met before. Being of Whig lineage, I had from
boyhood been taught to distrust and dislike Van
Buren and to believe in and admire Clay. The

first thing which struck me, as I studied the two
men, was Van Buren's evident superiority in
intellectual power. This was a disappointment,
and almost a shock to me. I could not bear to
think that this " tricky Democrat " could be in
any wise superior to "glorious Harry of the
West." On further study of the men, I was
comforted by the conviction that Clay possessed
the more eagle-like qualities, and that in public
debate and personal intellectual encounters Van
Buren would be no match for him. But I could
not divest myself of the impression that in a
contest carried on in writing, where personal
magnetism and oratorial powers could not be
brought into play, Clay would be no match for
Van Buren. Clay's manner was the more
instantaneously captivating ; but as the minutes
glided by, Van Buren constantly won upon the
favor of the company, and before he took his
leave he had gained a powerful hold upon their
respect and admiration. To me, his conversation, his gracefulness, his elegance, his perfect

equipoise, his exquisite courtesy, his intellectual grip on every subject he touched, were a revelation that filled me with wonder and delight.

I afterwards studied up Van Buren's history and made as thorough an analysis of his character as my opportunities permitted. Phrenologically speaking, his affectional and propelling organs were markedly developed. Love of home and family and friends was strong in him. His combativeness, destructiveness, caution and secretiveness were all very large. This gave him great energy and industry, with perfect mental and emotional equipoise and absolute self possession under all circumstances. His firmness, self-esteem, approbativeness and hope were large, giving him dignity and courtesy of demeanor, strength of purpose and elasticity of spirits. He was never long despondent under adversity. His moral organs were well developed, but his spiritual or religious faculties were weak ; and hence, while he was distinguished for uprightness of character and purity

of life, he was devoid of enthusiasm and destitute of emotional fervor. His intellectual faculties were massive and active. His brain was
large in every way—rather too large for his
body. His organ of language, though fairly
developed, was not large; and this defect, enhanced by his lack of warmth and enthusiasm,
prevented him from taking high rank as an
orator. But he was a clear and powerful
reasoner, and was adroit in presenting his cause
with all its strong points foremost.

Under his placid demeanor, Van Buren
could cherish a vehement desire to inflict what
theologians call "punitive justice" on his foes,
and was capable of pursuing a purpose with
tenacious determination when his feelings were
deeply enlisted in his own behalf. He was proud
and sensitive; and his pride and sensibility
had been deeply wounded by his treatment by
the Democratic party, and especially by what he
believed to be the deliberate treachery of General Cass. He was naturally on the side of Free-

soil.   He was in favor of the Wilmot Proviso.
He had long chafed under the lead of Southern
statesmen, to which his affiliations with the
Democratic party had compelled him to submit.

How aggravating that Southern lead was to
high-minded Northern statesmen, it is impossible
for people of this generation to imagine.   All
that the South had to do to concentrate its
entire influence against a Northern man was to
whisper that he was hostile to slavery.   If he
wavered a single jot or tittle in his allegiance to
the "peculiar institution," he was at once ostracised.   These tactics were brought into play
early in the history of our government.   Webster, in his reply to Hayne, away back in 1830,
pointedly alluded to this practice.   "I know full
well," he said, "that it is, and has been, the
settled policy of some persons in the South, for
years, to represent the people of the North as
disposed to interfere with them in their own
exclusive and peculiar concerns.   This is a delicate and sensitive point in Southern feeling ; and

of late years it has always been touched, and generally with effect, whenever the object has been to unite the whole South against Northern men and Northern measures. This feeling, always carefully kept alive, and maintained at too intense a heat to admit discrimination or reflection, is a lever of great power in our political machine."

The South did not attempt any disguise or concealment in this matter. Southern leaders made no secret of their tyrannical insistence. On the contrary, they gloried in it; and doubt-less, such of their descendants as shall read this narrative, will indulge in smiles of grim satisfaction and pride, on being reminded how, by means of such speedy and invincible concentration of Southern sentiment, their honored and beloved predecessors always compelled their Northern allies to lick the dust of humiliation.

In addition to other reasons, the implacable hatred of Van Buren by John C. Calhoun and his friends (which will be accounted for when we come to the delineation of Calhoun's character), had helped to make " New York's favorite son " feel his galling yoke of political servitude in all its bitterness. And now, the Democratic party, under the lead of the South, had insultingly cast him aside, and given its leadership to the man who had so cruelly betrayed him. Van Buren was in the 66th year of his age, and could not hope for any future political preferment. But he could throw off his political chains and strike an avenging and deadly blow at the false friend who had betrayed him, and at the party which had humiliated him. Was it in human nature for "a frail human brother"— to speak after the manner of good men— to forego such an opportunity for vengeance? Seward and Weed knew it was not; they understood the passions which were seething in Van Buren's soul, and took steps to utilize them for the defeat of Cass and the election of Taylor. They unobtrusively formed an alliance with Benjamin F. Butler, a distinguished lawyer in the city of New York, who was a leader in the Democratic party, and Van Buren's most intimate and trusted friend. Butler had been a pet and *protégé* of Van Buren's from his boyhood. He studied law in Van Buren's office at Kinderhook, and became his law partner at the age of twenty-two. During the last year of Van Buren's presidency, Butler was his acting Secretary of War ; and from the day that Van Buren left the White House, on March 4th, 1841, Butler had been devoted to him both politically and personally. He keenly felt what he believed to be the wrongs of his beloved chief, and burned to avenge them upon his foes.

VII. The Free-soil National Convention at Buffalo.

Butler had reason for believing that although Van Buren would not demean himself by leading a mere faction fight in the State of New York, he would not refuse to place himself at the head of a great national movement, and a great national movement had been determined upon. A call was issued for a National Convention of all those who were opposed to the extension of slavery into the new Territories, to meet at Buffalo, on the 9th day of August. All the States were invited to send delegates to the Convention, to nominate Free soil candidates for the Presidency and Vice Presidency. This movement received the enthusiastic support of the disaffected anti-slavery men in both parties, and also of the old line abolitionists. The Convention was attended by all the anti slavery magnates (except those who belonged to the extreme Garrisonian wing) and by thousands of the rank and file. There was a sprinkling of delegates from Delaware, Maryland and Virginia ; and one of the Virginia delegates electrified the Convention by announcing that he was " from the south of Mason's and *Dickenson's* line." I was in attendance to report the proceedings of the Convention for publication in pamphlet form.

When the Convention got under way, it was discovered that the preference for John P. Hale as the candidate of the party was strongly predominant and seemingly irresistible. To make matters worse, Van Buren coquetted with the Convention, and sent his friends a letter, in which he reminded them of his refusal to accept the nomination which was tendered to him at Utica in June, and strongly hinted that it would not be agreeable for him to be compelled to refuse another nomination. He put it delicately, and also adroitly, in these words :

"You know, from my letter to the Utica convention, and the confidence you repose in my sincerity, how greatly the proceedings of that body, in relation to myself, were opposed to my earnest wishes."

This letter was received as conclusive by the friends of John P. Hale. They considered his nomination as good as made ; and in their blind confidence, they made the same mistake which the friends of Clay had made two months before at Philadelphia. They hurrahed, made speeches—fiery, eloquent, excellent speeches— and seemed to be having everything their own way. Meanwhile, Seward, Weed and Butler, who read Van Buren's letter with a native sagacity of perception which their own long practice in writing similar letters had sharpened to an almost preternatural keenness, were effectively working to head off Hale and bring Van Buren to the front. Seward and Weed, of course, worked secretly ; Butler openly. They knew that the proceedings of " that body "—the Utica convention, which represented only a sec- tion of a party in a single State, was quite a different thing, in Van Buren's estimation, from the proceedings of a great National Con- vention under the control of some of the most conspicuous and influential men in the country.

It being certain that if the Convention should come to an early vote, Hale would be nominated, a good deal of preliminary business was introduced, and opportunity was given to

every ardent orator to orate as long as he
pleased. When the names of candidates were
proposed, Hon. Henry Dodge, U. S. Senator
from Wisconsin, who was a highly respected
Free-soiler, was put forward as the opponent of
Hale. Dodge was very popular in the West,
and his name was greeted with such enthusiasm, it seemed as though he would carry off
the prize. Charles Francis Adams was also
named as a candidate for the Presidency, and
his name was received with such hearty cheers
that the Hale men were bewildered. A message soon came from Senator Dodge, requesting
his friends to withdraw his name, and assign-
ing ill health as a reason why it would be
impossible for him to accept the burdens of the
candidacy. It was then proposed—the idea
being started by the secret friends of Van
Buren—that Hale should be nominated for the
Presidency and Dodge for the Vice-Presidency.
This proposition was opposed by the friends of
Adams. It was also opposed by the avowed

friends of Van Buren, who were seeking to gain time, perplex counsel, weary patience, and get the Convention into such a frame of mind as would lead to the adoption of their plan when it should be presented. After a while, another communication was received from Senator Dodge, refusing to allow his name to be presented to the Convention for any purpose whatever. This was a set back to the friends of Hale and helped to complicate still more the already confused state of things.

And now, when everything seemed to be at cross-purposes, the friends of Van Buren played their winning card. It was proposed, in order to simplify matters, and maintain that harmony which should characterize the deliberations of freemen met to carry out a great and holy cause, that a committee on nominations should be appointed, who could consult calmly and quietly upon the situation, come to definite conclusions, and report the same to the Convention, for its approval or rejection, as the case

might be. This proposition was adopted, and
the committee on nominations was appointed.
What the views of a majority of that committee
were, it is easy to imagine, when it is remembered that Butler and his helpers knew just
exactly what they were about, and that the
friends of Hale were taken unawares by the
proposition. The committee went into secret
session. Butler was a member of it, and so
was Salmon P. Chase, the President of the
Convention, who up to that time had been a
Van Buren Democrat, and who didn't like Hale
nearly as well as he liked Chase.

Butler soon took the lead in the committee.
He had made elaborate and profound preparation for this very crisis, and his management
was so consummately able that it would have
excited the admiration of Van Buren himself,
could he have witnessed it. He first convinced
the committee that Van Buren would accept
the nomination, if it were unanimously tendered to him. Then he set at work to persuade

them that Van Buren was nothing less than a providential candidate. Here was a man who for more than a generation had enjoyed the confidence of his countrymen ; who had filled every official position, from a State legislator to President of the United States, with conspic- uous ability and integrity ; whose name was known and honored throughout the civilized world—this great, good and renowned man they could now have for their standard bearer in the desperate contest in which they were about to engage for the cause which was so dear to their hearts. His appeal was successful. The com- mittee began to be satisfied that it would give them national *prestige* to have Van Buren for their candidate. Butler then discoursed upon Van Buren's admirable personal character, and in winning words set forth the purity and vir- tues of his private life. He gave an animated and picturesque description of a visit he had recently made him, at his home in Kinderhook. As he was describing the almost boyish activity

with which Van Buren went over his farm, and
the pride he took in his fields of grain and cabbages and turnips, a tall, gaunt delegate from
Ohio, named Brinkerhoff, slowly and spirally
elevating himself like a jackscrew, shrieked out,
in shrill, piercing tones :

" Damn his cabbages and turnips! What
does he say about the abolition of slavery in the
Deestrick of Columby !"

This was a thunderclap. Silence reigned,
but not long. The committee spontaneously
burst into a roar of mingled laughter and
cheers.

To understand the terrific impact of that
question, it should be remembered that only
eleven years before (March 4, 1837), in his in-
augural address, Van Buren, quoting from his
letter accepting the nomination to the Presidency, had said :

" I must go into the Presidential chair the
inflexible and uncompromising opponent of
every attempt on the part of Congress to

abolish slavery in the District of Columbia against the wishes of the slaveholding States."

The explosion of such an interrogative bombshell as Brinkerhoff hurled at Van Buren's eulogist would have utterly disconcerted an ordinary speaker. But the veteran Butler was equal to the occasion, and turned what might have been a disaster into a means of triumph. Thanking his "friend from Ohio" for thus bringing forward the important subject of the abolition of slavery in the District of Columbia, he would answer, from personal knowledge of the views and convictions of Mr. Van Buren on that subject, that if he should be elected President of the United States, and if a bill abolishing slavery in the District of Columbia should be passed by Congress, it would receive the President's signature. This assurance occasioned great enthusiasm and was received with prolonged applause and cheers. The feeling thus excited decided the contest in the committee. It was unanimously resolved to recommend Martin Van Buren to the Convention as the Free-soil candidate for the Presidency, and Charles Francis Adams for Vice-President. A platform of principles was also prepared, which was so extreme in its expression of Free-soil and anti-slavery views that it could not fail to satisfy the most uncompromising members of the party. The Convention adopted the report of the committee entire, both as to candidates and platform, and Van Buren and Adams were nominated with enthusiasm.

One of the mottoes put forth in the platform as a party cry, was: "No more slave States ; no more slave Territories." Soon after its adoption, Salmon P. Chase arose and said it was thought best to amend the platform in one respect, namely : Instead of having it read "No more slave States ; no more slave Territories," it was proposed to strike out the word "more" in the last clause, so the motto would be : "No *more* slave States ; *no* slave Territories." Nothing which occurred during the sitting of the Convention occasioned more intense enthusiasm than did this proposed amendment. For some reason it seemed to touch the inmost heart of the delegates and the spectators, and it was adopted with prolonged cheering.

Van Buren and Adams at once accepted their nominations, and the Free-soilers, joyously throwing their banner to the breeze, went into the campaign with wild hurrahs, shouting their motto, "No *more* slave States ; *no* slave Territories."

VIII. The Triangular Fight for the Presidency—Public Feeling in Washington.

The ensuing triangular contest for the Presidency was an exceedingly embittered one. The spectacle of Martin Van Buren—"New York's favorite son"—leading the anti-slavery hosts to battle was inexpressibly maddening to the Democrats, especially to those of the South, and they fairly thirsted for the blood of the

Free-soilers. The friends of Henry Clay could not forgive his alleged betrayal. The candidacy of General Taylor did not evoke any party enthusiasm. Daniel Webster said that his nomination was one not fit to be made. Horace Greeley held aloof week after week, and as it was becoming apparent that the vote of New York State would probably decide the contest, his action caused great consternation. In this emergency it was reported and believed that the gallant Clay, although he would not take an active part in the campaign, earnestly desired the triumph of the Whig cause. This conciliated many of Clay's friends. Webster, not that he disliked Taylor less, but that he hated Cass and Van Buren more, was induced to address a mass meeting at Marshfield, in support of the Whig cause.

His speech was a masterly one. He analyzed the situation to the very bottom, and exhibited the practical issues at stake in the election in the clearest light. No address could possibly have been better adapted to persuade disaffected Whigs to return to the party ranks and vote the regular ticket. It was widely published, and produced a profound effect throughout the Northern States. Greeley so hated the Democratic party that he could not keep out of the fight. He was nominated for a short term in Congress, and threw himself and the *Tribune* into the campaign with his accustomed ardor and energy. Everything began to work, especially in New York, which was the pivotal State, as Seward and Weed had foreseen. As the contest went on, and the deeper feelings of the partisans were stirred, the anti-slavery Whigs of the Empire State discovered that they could not play into the hands of the Barnburners by voting for Martin Van Buren. Thousands of them returned to their party allegiance, and cast their votes for Taylor and Fillmore. This decided the contest. Aside from the vote of New York, Taylor had 128 and Cass 127 electoral votes. The vote of New York then—

as so often before and since—determined on which banner victory should perch ; and, owing to the vast Democratic bolt in favor of Van Buren, Taylor got the vote of the Empire State, by a small plurality, which gave him 37 majority in the Electoral College—and carried the Whig party again, and for the last time, into Federal power.

It was only a month after this bitter contest was ended that the session of Congress began, and the animosities and heartburnings which had been engendered by the fight were carried to Washington. On the fifth day of the ensuing March—the fourth coming on Sunday—General Taylor was to be inaugurated, and a Whig Administration, with an anti-slavery Vice-President to preside over the Senate, was to come into power. It was understood that William H. Seward, of New York, and Salmon P. Chase, of Ohio, were to be elected United States Senators from their respective States. Seward and Chase were detested by the South,

and the idea that they were to come into the
Senate was intolerable to some of the Southern
Senators. In addition to all these irritating
influences, an exasperating rumor was circulated that Seward had won the confidence of
General Taylor—who spoke of him as "the
great Mr. Seeward, of New York"—and would
be influential in shaping his administration.
All these things helped to increase the excitement with regard to slavery and abolition,
which already ran so high that it had occasioned mobs in Boston, in New York, and in
Philadelphia. Anti-slavery meetings were
often interrupted by mobs in New York. I was
present, as a reporter, at several such interruptions, and on one occasion had my hand trodden
upon by a ruffian who leaped upon the table at
which I was writing. Sometimes the tables
would be overturned and the legs torn out for
bludgeons. As we reporters were young and
enthusiastic in our profession, and were
endowed with a fair talent for table leg, we

sometimes got in a little good, concussive work on the *crania* of the disturbers of our peace and our notes.

In Washington, moderate anti slavery men were socially ostracised in slave holding circles, an abolitionist's life was sometimes believed to be in danger, and personal collisions were perpetually imminent. It was rumored that the Southern leaders had concerted a scheme for the introduction of slavery into the new Territories. This greatly excited the opponents of slavery extension, and they determined to oppose and defeat the alleged scheme at all hazards ; and it was in the collisions which it was expected would occur in the strife upon this subject, that the statesmen of that day apprehended danger to the country.

Such was the political and social situation at Washington, on the opening of the second session of the Thirtieth Congress, on December 4th, 1848.

CHAPTER II.

HALF-A-DOZEN NOTED SENATORS.

I. GENERAL SAM HOUSTON. —In 1848 there were thirty States in the Union and sixty Senators in Congress. Of all these sixty Senators but three are now (May, 1889) living, so far as I know; and they are Hannibal Hamlin, of Maine; Simon Cameron,* of Pennsylvania; and Jefferson Davis, of Mississippi.

The four men of whom I intend to write particularly are Calhoun, Benton, Clay and Webster. Clay was not in the Senate in 1848, but he came in at the session of '49.

Besides these four pre-eminently conspicuous men, there were others in the Senate deserving

* Cameron died June 28th, fifty days after the above was written.

of notice. There was General Sam Houston, of
Texas, about whose name more romance clus-
tered at that time than encircled the name of
any other American citizen. Houston was born
in ~~North Carolina~~ in 1793, but went to Tennessee while a boy. He became a popular favorite
at an early age, and after a brilliant military
and legal career, he entered the arena of politics,
and was elected Governor of Tennessee when he
was thirty-four years old. It was predicted that
he would be President of the United States before
he was fifty, but a sudden and incomprehensible
stroke of fortune shattered his career and drove
him from civilization.

The mystery which surrounded this misfor-
tune has never been authoritatively cleared up.
Shortly after his inauguration as Governor of
Tennessee, Houston married a beautiful young
lady ; and the legend is that at the time of her
marriage she had a lover (not Houston) to whom
she was passionately devoted ; that her family
compelled her to marry Houston because he

was Governor of Tennessee and the most popular man in the State except General Jackson ;
that Houston soon discovered the truth of the
matter and was overwhelmed by it—in fact,
was nearly driven insane by it. At all events,
he resigned his office and disappeared. It is said
that he did this in order that his wife might get
a divorce and marry the man she loved. After
a while it was found that he had gone to the
Cherokee country, had been made a chief of that
tribe, and was living in barbaric dignity ; that
is to say, in a wigwam plentifully supplied with
skins, wild game, whiskey and tobacco.

When the troubles between Texas and
Mexico began, Houston went to Texas, became
commander-in-chief of her army, defeated and
captured Santa Anna, in April, 1836, was elected
President of the Texan Republic, and finally,
when in 1845 Texas was annexed by treaty to
the United States, he was elected United States
Senator, and was a member of the Senate at the
period of which I am writing.

It is not probable that any one in these days feels, or could feel such an interest in General Houston as people, and especially young men, felt in him forty years ago. The tragic circumstances which attended the struggle of Texas for her independence were then fresh in our memories. My heart leaps now and my blood grows hot as I recall the time, in April, 1836, when the news of the terrible fight in the Alamo, at San Antonio de Bexar, first came to the sequestered village of Lockport, N. Y., where I lived, then a boy just coming twelve years old. I wept over the fate of the three heroic colonels—Travis, Crockett and Bowie, and young as I was I thirsted for vengeance and prayed for vengeance on their slayers.

As we children on the Niagara frontier were brought up to hate the British, wild beasts, Indians, and foes of every kind whatso·ever, and were taught to believe in the good old-fashioned fire and brimstone hell, and in cognate Scripture tenets, undiluted with any revisionary

Sheol or Hades, I suppose that our militant
religion had a robustness and an edge which
are impossible to the faith of boys brought up
on the humanitarianism and the diluted the-
ology of the present day. At any rate, we all
prayed fervently to God to avenge Travis,
Crockett and Bowie on the Mexicans. And
when, four or five weeks afterwards, news
came of the massacre of Colonel Fannin and his
men at Goliad, after they had surrendered
under a solemn agreement, in writing, that
they should be treated as prisoners of war, the
whole community was aroused to madness.
Public meetings were held and fiery resolutions
were passed. We prayed for vengeance more
fervently than ever. Twenty-four boys, of
which I was one, formed a company to march
down and ravage Mexico; but news of Houston's defeat and capture of Santa Anna at San
Jacinto came in time to save that ill-fated
republic from the impending invasion.

The battle of San Jacinto was fought in

April, but news of the victory did not reach
Lockport till June. There were no railroads or
telegraphs in those days (1836). But it did not
make any difference. The news was just as
fresh and welcome when it came, as though it
had been flashed over the wires on the day of
battle. We all rejoiced with exceeding great
joy, felt proud to think that our prayers for
vengeance had been answered so soon, and
took great comfort in our religion which so
speedily led to such gratifying and practical
results. We were a simple people who believed
in God, and loved heroes who won battles in
accordance with our prayers; and from that
time General Sam Houston was set in our
hearts alongside Jackson and Washington.

Twelve years had passed, and I was now to
see this hero face to face, to hear him speak,
and report his words. My experience with
"great men" and politicians at the Whig Convention the previous June, and at the Free-soil
Convention in August, had rather chilled my

expectations as to all sorts of heroes.   Hence it
was not without apprehension that I first
approached General Houston and looked him
over, as he stood in an ante-room of the Senate
Chamber, talking with his colleague, Senator
Rusk.   I was not disappointed in his appearance.   It was easy to believe in his heroism, and
to imagine him leading a heady fight, and
dealing destruction on his foes.   He was then
only fifty-five years old, and seemed to be in
perfect health and admirable physical condition.
He was a magnificent barbarian, somewhat
tempered with civilization.   He was large of
frame, of stately carriage and dignified
demeanor, and had a lionlike countenance capable of expressing the fiercest passions.   His
dress was peculiar, but it was becoming to his
style.   The conspicuous features of it were a
military cap, and a short military cloak of fine
blue broadcloath, with a blood-red lining.
Afterwards, I occasionally met him when he
wore a vast and picturesque sombrero and a

Mexican blanket—a sort of ornamented bed-quilt, with a slit in the middle, through which the wearer's head is thrust, leaving the blanket to hang in graceful folds around the body.

Like other men of his class, General Houston was a heavy drinker, but he seldom showed the effect of his potations. It seemed to me as though his wild life had unfitted him for civilization. He was not a man to shine in a deliberative assembly. It was only at rare intervals that he took any part in the debates, and when he did speak, his remarks were brief. His principal employment in the Senate was whittling pine sticks. I used to wonder where he got his pine lumber, but never fathomed the mystery. He would sit and whittle away, and at the same time keep up a muttering of discontent at the long winded speakers, whom he would sometimes curse for their intolerable verbosity. Those who knew him well said that he was tender hearted, and had a chivalric regard for women ; that he would make any personal

sacrifice to promote the welfare of a lady friend
—a reputation which was directly in line with
his alleged conduct towards his wife. It was a
matter of common jocose remark that if "Old
San Jacinto" (that was Houston's nickname)
should ever become President, he would have a
Cabinet of women.

General Houston impressed me as a lonely,
melancholy man. And if the story of his early
life was true, he might well be lonely and
melancholy, notwithstanding his success and
his fame ; for that terrible blow which smote
him to the heart at the zenith of his splendid
young career, and dislocated his life, and drove
him to the wilderness, must have inflicted
wounds that no political triumphs or military
glory could heal. He was a sincere lover of his
country, was indomitably patriotic, and stood
firmly by the Union to the day of his death,
which came in 1863.

II. JEFFERSON DAVIS.

Another member of that Senatorial body who deserves notice was Jefferson Davis, whose subsequent career has made his name known throughout the civilized world. Mr. Davis was son-in-law to General Taylor, the incoming President. He was forty years old (1848) and in vigorous health, but lame from a wound he received only twenty-one months before, in the Mexican war, in which he greatly distinguished himself. Indeed, his gallant conduct at the desperate battle of Buena Vista, where he received his wound, had made him, next to Scott and Taylor, one of the most popular heroes of the day.

I have spoken of the excitement caused in Lockport on the reception of the news of the tragic events which occurred during the Texan war for independence. A similar, but a much deeper excitement was felt throughout the entire country, with regard to the fate of General

Taylor and his army, for several weeks before authentic news of the battle of Buena Vista was received. It was reported that Taylor's forces had been greatly reduced by the mismanagement of the Administration at Washington, and that "Old Rough and Ready," as General Taylor was affectionately nicknamed, had been purposely left to be destroyed to prevent his coming into the field as a Whig candidate for the Presidency. This rumor was, of course, cruelly false, but it was believed, and gave additional intensity to the interest which was felt in the uncertain fate of the old hero. It became known that Santa Anna, seeing his opportunity, had rushed to Taylor's destruction with an overwhelming force. Our little army was beyond the reach of all ordinary channels of communication, and so the country was left in terrible suspense as to its fate. The ear of the nation was turned with agonizing solicitude to catch the first tidings from that devoted little band. And when the news at last came—the news of a bloody victory—gained after two days of desperate fighting against overwhelming odds—it came with a rush and a roar and an outburst of rejoicing, such as the country had never before witnessed or heard. The news was brought across Texas to New Orleans by pony express, and was conveyed through the country by the same slow means, except where navigable rivers gave an opportunity to send it by steamboat. As the newspaper reporters and the bearers of dispatches scurried through the country they told the news along their routes, and the entire population broke out with rejoicing in their wake. City after city, village after village, hamlet after hamlet was illuminated, and the whole nation revelled in rejoicing. Every particular of the battle was minutely described, and the descriptions were eagerly read. Among these descriptions was a glowing account of the gallantry of Colonel Jefferson Davis of the First Regiment of Mississippi Volunteers, who, though badly wounded, refused to quit the field, but grimly sat on his horse at the head of his regiment, and held a vital position against a vastly superior force, until victory was assured.

Colonel Davis, who was a graduate of West Point and had served several years in the regular army, was an accomplished soldier. His regiment, the First Mississippi, was attacked by a force that outnumbered it six to one, and was sorely pressed. But Davis, knowing that if they were driven from their position the American line of battle would be so weakened as to imperil the safety of the entire army, held his ground with invincible resolution. When he was so badly wounded that the surgeon told him he must retire, he refused to go. He had his wound dressed while he sat in his saddle, and held on. Santa Anna, growing desperate at the successful resistance of the Mississippians, finally ordered a brigade of cavalry to charge them. Davis, seeing what was coming, formed his regiment in the shape of a V, opening towards the enemy, while he sat at its apex. According to the descriptions of the battle published at the time, the Mexicans came gallantly on and rode into the V. The Mississippians stood with their rifles at their shoulders and their fingers on the triggers, awaiting the orders of their colonel. When Davis saw that the critical moment had come, his clarion voice rang out the one word, "Fire!" His troops spontaneously responded, and blew the Mexicans from their saddles. The end soon came. The surviving foes, appalled by the slaughter, galloped wildly from the field; the victorious Mississippians had a respite from their desperate struggle, and their sorely wounded colonel was able to seek the relief which he so much needed. It was the wound thus and then received which caused the lameness of Jefferson Davis when I first saw him in Washington, in December, 1848.

Mr. Davis was a handsome man, with a symmetrical figure, well up to the medium size,

a piercing but kindly eye, and a gamy, chivalric bearing. He had a fine, sonorous voice,
and was always a fluent and sometimes an
eloquent speaker. He was ready and skillful
in debate, animated in style, occasionally
vehement in manner, but always courteous.

I—then a young man of twenty-four, and
only a few years out of the woods of Niagara
county—became attached to Jefferson Davis, on
account of his genial personal kindness.
Sometimes there were bills before the Senate
full of Indian names, or Mexican (Aztec) names,
or Spanish names, that the Senators could not
pronounce correctly and which we reporters
could not catch ; hence, it was necessary for us
to get sight of the names in print, in order to
write them out correctly in our reports. Whenever a discussion on such a bill took place, I
used to apply to Mr. Davis for a copy of the
document, and he would always get me one, no
matter how much trouble it gave him to do so.
And he did it with such genial courtesy and

kindness that'his manner went straight to the heart and stayed there. In fact, I used to notice that it seemed to give Jefferson Davis pleasure to do an act of kindness for anybody.

It is not probable that Mr. Davis remembers any of these things (or that he even remembers my name), but they are fresh in my recollection. ¡I often thought of Mr. Davis's kind personal traits in after years, and especially during the war, when any of us Northern men would have been glad to have had him slain as an enemy of the country, which sentiment he doubtless fully and naturally reciprocated. But now that all that is past, and the asperities of war have given place to the amenities of peace, I find only friendly feelings in my heart towards Jefferson Davis, and would gladly reciprocate, if opportunity should offer, the kindness which, all those years ago, he showed to me, an obscure young man. when he was a distinguished and powerful Senator of the United States.

III. John P. Hale.

John P. Hale, of New Hampshire, was the first man who was elected a United States Senator on a square anti-slavery issue. It was reported that when Hale first took his seat in the Senate, his life was threatened by pro-slavery fanatics. This may have been true; for, although no Southern man of distinction would have thought of making or of countenancing such a threat, there has never been any age or any party in which, if there was a chance for an act of folly to be committed, there was not some fool on hand ready to commit it. An attempt was certainly made to browbeat Hale into silence ; but the effort was ludicrously futile. It might as well have been attempted to silence the thunder of Niagara.

A Methodist minister in New Hampshire said that " John P. Hale had been specially selected by Providence to inoculate the Senate of the United States with the spirit and practice of free speech on the subject of slavery." I do not know that the Methodist minister was in the confidence of Providence, and so spoke by the card ; but Hale's career as a Senator showed that if he, in fact, was thus commissioned, Providence exhibited its usual sagacity when it chose him for the alleged purpose.

Hale was thoroughly brave, and always stood up manfully for his rights ; but he was so constitutionally good-natured that he could not be provoked to anger, and so incorrigibly lazy, it was impossible to stimulate him into a row. In addition to these amiable qualities, he had an inexhaustible fund of unctuous humor and brilliant wit. His voice was a pleasant, penetrating tenor, his enunciation was distinct, and he spoke with extraordinary fluency. He had a genius for debate. Nobody in the Senate could successfully contend with him in repartee.

Senator Foote, of Mississippi (a loquacious and good-natured man, who sometimes let his tongue say what his heart would repudiate),

permitted himself to declare, on the floor of the
Senate, that if the abolitionist, Hale, should
ever come to Mississippi, they would hang him
there on the tallest tree that could be found.
This shocked the Senate (and in fact the whole
country), and Southern Senators disclaimed
sympathy with such an unparliamentary utter-
ance. But Hale good-naturedly replied that if
the Senator from Mississippi should visit New
Hampshire, the intelligent and Christian people
of that State would not hang him, but would
treat him hospitably ; would show him their
churches and manufactories, their free schools
and free laborers, and do all possible missionary
work on him ; and if he still remained incorri-
ble, they would not hang him, but would hire a
hall for him, and let him talk as long as he
pleased, feeling certain that if they only gave
him rope enough, he would be sure to hang
himself. This good-natured and witty retort
was received with great laughter, in which
Senator Foote heartily joined. Hale invariably

got the laugh on anybody who attacked him ; and he finally became a favorite speaker with the majority of his Senatorial colleagues.

IV. STEPHEN A. DOUGLAS.

Stephen A. Douglas, of Illinois, had been in the Senate less than two years, in 1848, but he had begun to take rank as one of the foremost debaters in that body. He had a full and rich voice, was fluent in speech, but spoke with deliberation and perfect distinctness of enunciation, and was thoroughly self-possessed. Mr. Douglas was called " The Little Giant," but he was not a little man. He was short in stature, but he was broad-shouldered and deep-chested, and had a large and finely developed head. I used to think that his head, though smaller than Webster's, was modelled after the same pattern.

Mr. Douglas's manner, though easy and utterly unconstrained, was dignified and urbane. Sometimes, when he was speaking with animation, he had a good natured, earnest, lionlike look, blended with the utmost simplicity and illuminated with a high degree of intelligence. On such an occasion, I doubt if a stranger, who heard him for the first time and did not even know his name, could have listened to him ten minutes without being strongly attracted by his engaging manner, nor without at least beginning to feel a personal regard for him. He was still more winning in private intercourse. There was not the least taint of snobbishness about him : he was utterly devoid of pretentiousness. He never put on what vain and self-conscious Senators imagine to be airs of Senatorial dignity. His dignity was of that solid, genuine, American sort which can unconsciously take care of itself without airs of any kind.

Mr. Douglas was fond of young men and young men liked him. His easy, familiar, friendly manner was always impressive but never oppressive. Several times he had occasion, or else he pretended to have occasion, to speak to me while I was in the reporter's seat (then several feet at the left of the Vice-President's chair), during a lull in the business of the Senate. Every time he thus spoke to me, he laid his arm upon my shoulder in a companionable way, and talked as though I were a younger brother in whom he took an affectionate interest. A long time afterwards, when Douglas had been several years in his grave, I met an enthusiastic friend of his in Mankato, Minnesota, who had risen to political distinction ; and on describing his first meeting, when a young man, with Douglas, at a party in Chicago, he spoke of this same manner, and told me how it thrilled him, and won his heart forever, when the distinguished Senator laid his arm caressingly upon his shoulder and spoke to him with friendly interest and paternal benignity.

Douglas died in 1861. I never saw him after 1850.

V. SIMON CAMERON.

Senator Cameron impressed me as one of the most knowing men in the Senate. Mentally and physically he was energetic, active, alert. He was a good debater. He always spoke clearly and to the point. He never wasted any words. As John P. Hale said, "he had a boring-in style, like an augur." He was a Pennsylvania Tariff Democrat, and was aggressive in asserting his opinions and convictions. He brought on the first debate of the Session by opposing a motion made by Senator Davis, of Mississippi, to print twenty thousand extra copies of the report of the Secretary of the Treasury.

Robert J. Walker, of Mississippi, was Secretary of the Treasury, and one of the leaders in the free-trade crusade of that time, which culminated in the repeal of the Whig protective tariff of 1842, and the enactment of the Democratic revenue tariff of 1846. His report contained an elaborate disquisition on the advantages of the financial policy which had thus been inaugurated.

Senator Cameron said he didn't believe the country wanted any extra copies of the Secretary's report. Referring to the defeat of the Democratic party in the recent election, he said "he thought that the country had already decided on the merits of the Secretary's system of finance, and they had decided against it." His remarks occasioned an outburst of indignation on the part of Democratic Senators, and the discussion soon became heated. Senator Hale, seizing the opportunity to let off a little of his witty nonsense, said :

" He was surprised to learn from the Senator from Pennsylvania, that the people of this country, in the late Presidential election, had decided against the late tariff act, and in favor of that of 1842. As he understood it, the one great question connected with that election was, whether General Taylor or either of the

other nominees was the most genuine Free-
soil man.   And it was generally conceded that
General Taylor was the genuine, Simon Pure
Free-soil candidate, while Mr. Van Buren and his
friends were held as mere pretenders and inter-
lopers."   [Laughter.]

Hale's jocosity, although it led to a brief
diversion of the debate from the tariff to the
recent Presidential election, did not turn the
free-trade Democrats from their pursuit of the
offending Senator from Pennsylvania.   They
soon returned to their attacks on him, and to
the support of the motion to print an extra
number of Secretary Walker's free-trade
report.   The Whig Senators were, of course,
delighted at this domestic infelicity in the ranks
of their opponents, and some of them good-
naturedly helped it on by taking sides with
Cameron.   But that belligerent Senator did not
need any help.   He easily held his own, and
dealt blows right and left, with such vigor as
made the debate uncomfortable for his party.

In a sharp rejoinder to observations made by some of the Southern Democrats, he said :

"In my State, (Pennsylvania,) where the people live by their honest industry, where every man works, and subsists upon the labor of his own hands, there the tariff was the question which was discussed, the issue that was placed before the people. The Democratic party would not have been prostrated had it not been for this financial system."

But Cameron's opposition to the printing of twenty thousand extra copies of Secretary Walker's free-trade report was futile. The motion to print was carried by a vote of 29 to 21.

The reporters felt grateful to Cameron for bringing on this debate. They were paid a stipend of ten dollars a week, and four dollars a column for their reports. A week of the session had passed without any debate, and all the compensation the reporters had received was their weekly stipend of ten dollars. It may be imagined, therefore, how delighted they were to have a debate brought on which put many shekels in their purses.

Cameron was always friendly to the report-ers. On one occasion, when Senator Badger, of North Carolina, introduced a resolution " that the Committee on Printing inquire into the expediency of discontinuing the contract made at the last session for publishing the reports of the debates and proceedings of Congress," he spoke warmly and emphatically in favor of the reporters. The contract to which Senator Bad-ger's resolution referred, was made with the *National Intelligencer,* the organ of the Whig party, and the *Union,* the organ of the Demo-cratic party. Each of those papers was paid seven dollars a column for its Congressional reports. The proprietors of the papers inter-preted their contract so liberally that they included everything which came before Con-gress––President's messages, reports of heads of Departments, and public documents of every

kind—in " The debates and proceedings," and
published them at seven dollars a column. This
occasioned a good deal of dissatisfaction. In
addition to this, some of the Senators were
indignant because their speeches did not read as
well in print as they would have liked them to
read. There was an extended debate on the
resolution, which was finally narrowed down to
an animated discussion of the ability and faith-
fulness of the reporters. On this question
Senator Cameron spoke out with vigor and appreciation.

"I do not believe," he said, "there is a
better set of men in the world, in their profession, than those who are now engaged in
reporting our debates. They are highly
educated, talented, and accomplished, and they
devote more time to their profession here than
any class of men engaged in any other profession in the world devote to labor."

The reporters all liked Senator Cameron.
The system of reporting the Congressional

debates was continued without modification, or any more fault-finding.

Senator Cameron had the reputation of possessing the Jacksonian virtue of standing inflexibly by his friends. He also had the Jacksonian pluck and grit, as Senator Foote, of Mississippi, discovered on a memorable occasion. It was the last night of the Thirtieth Congress, March 3, 1849, when the session of the Senate was prolonged till seven o'clock on Sunday morning. Some of the members took the ground that the Thirtieth Congress went out of existence at the hour of midnight, and that Senators whose term of office expired with the termination of Congress (of whom Cameron was one) ceased to be Senators at midnight, and had no right to take part in the proceedings of the Senate after that hour. That prolonged session wore out the patience of many Senators, and violent outbursts of ill-temper repeatedly occurred. Senator Foote was especially aggravating in his manner towards members whose terms, as he alleged, had expired, and his conduct finally led to a disgraceful scene. About three o'clock on Sunday morning, while Senator Berrien, of Georgia, was speaking, there suddenly arose—I now copy from the report :

[Cries of " Question ! question ! question !"]

MR. BERRIEN. Who calls question ?

MR. FOOTE. It is parliamentary to do so.

MR. HANNEGAN. When I said " question " I thought the Senator from Georgia had taken his seat.

MR. CAMERON. I called for the question, because I was astonished that men holding the high and responsible station of Senators of the United States —

MR. FOOTE. I call the Senator from Pennsylvania to order. He has no right to talk here, still less to interrupt other Senators. His term of office has expired.

*   *   *   *   *

MR. CAMERON. I rise to a point of order. I wish to know whether such language is parliamentary.

MR. FOOTE. It is very proper under the circumstances.

MR. CAMERON. I did not ask his opinion. I can judge for myself. sir, of what is right and proper.

[Other words were uttered by both the Senators from Pennsylvania and Mississippi, and something approaching a personal collision ensued.]

That is the polite and euphemistic way in which the report puts it ; but the plain truth of the matter was that the two Senators called each other opprobrious names and then clinched. As General Houston said : " The eloquent and impassioned gentlemen got into each other's hair." They were soon separated, but not until it became apparent that the Keystone State had the better man in the field, and he was not molested again.

Mr. Cameron's subsequent career forms a part of the country's history. He always had devoted friends who loved to celebrate his virtues, but were sometimes indiscreet in their expressions of admiration. For example : When Cameron resigned his office as Secretary of War, in 1862, a Pennsylvania editor gave him two columns of eulogy, winding up with a burst of equivocal enthusiasm. " Thirty years ago," said the ardent editor, " Simon Cameron landed from a raft at Harrisburgh, with only a dime in his pocket, and yesterday he

left the War Office worth five millions of
dollars."

VI. HANNIBAL HAMLIN.

Mr. Hamlin is the youngest of the three (or,
since Mr. Cameron's recent death, of the two)
survivors of the sixty Senators of 1848. He
was born August 27, 1809; Jefferson Davis,
June 3, 1808 ; Simon Cameron, March 8, 1799.

Mr. Hamlin's distinguished career has made
his name and his history familiar to his countrymen. I do not remember that I ever spoke to
him, and he so seldom took part in the Senatorial debates that my observation of him was
too slight to fix his individuality clearly in my
recollection. I remember, however, two convictions which his appearance impressed upon
me ; one of which was that he was a man of
absolute honesty and uprightness ; the other,
that he was a genial and humorous man. I
remember thinking that he must be a good
story teller, and that he would be a pleasant
companion with whom to pass an afternoon or

evening on the deck of a steamboat, or on the piazza of a hotel at a summer resort.

There were other men in the Senate at this period who were then notable personages. But there is not sufficient surviving public interest in them to warrant me in sketching them here. They did not happen to do anything under my observation, or say anything in my hearing which was noteworthy, and as I never gave them particular attention, I have only a vague recollection of their personal characteristics. I will therefore pass on to the delineation of the four great Senators—Calhoun, Benton, Clay and Webster—of whose characters and personalities I have made special and prolonged study.

VII. Alexander H. Stephens—An Incident at Judge McLean's.

Before entering upon the delineation of the character of Calhoun, Benton, Clay and Webster, I will refer to a distinguished member of the House of Representatives—Alexander H.

Stephens, of Georgia—because of an incident
which has a bearing on a matter of some importance which was subsequently discussed by
Calhoun.

The Honorable John McLean, of Ohio, one
of the Justices of the United States Supreme
Court, and his wife became so interested in
phonography, the new system of short-hand
writing, then coming into vogue, that they
arranged for me to give a lecture upon the subject in their parlors. They invited a distinguished company to hear the lecture. Mr.
Stephens was present. After I had explained
the system, and (with the aid of a blackboard)
taught the audience to read simple sentences
written in phonographic characters, an exhibition of rapid writing was given by Dennis F.
Murphy, who for many years has been the
most accomplished reporter in the United States
Senate, but was then a pupil of mine, fourteen
years old. The first thing which was read for
Murphy to take down in short-hand was a pas-

sage from the Declaration of Independence. When the exercises were concluded, and Murphy had finished reading the dictated passage from his phonographic notes, Mr. Stephens asked :

"How old is that boy ?"

"Fourteen years," I replied.

"Then that is no test," he said. "Before I was fourteen years old, I knew the Declaration of Independence and the Constitution of the United States by heart. Read something else for the boy to write down."

Several passages from newspapers and books were read. Murphy, who had a remarkable gift for rapid writing, took them down with ease, and read them correctly from his notes, for which he was much applauded. As the company was dispersing, the Hon. Thomas Ewing, of Ohio (who came into General Taylor's cabinet a few months afterwards, as Secretary of the Interior), jocularly remarked to the Representative from Georgia :

"Stephens, you must have been a precocious boy to have known the Declaration of Independence and the Constitution of the United States by heart before you were fourteen years old."

" Oh, no ! " Stephens replied. " My school-fellows were equally familiar with them. We were brought up on those documents, and knew them sentence by sentence."

"Do any of you know them by heart now ?" asked Ewing.

"I can speak only for myself, as to that," Stephens answered. " I do not know that I could repeat them verbatim now, but I could come pretty near it."

A few days afterwards, I met Mr. Ewing ; and the phonographic lecture and Master Murphy's wonderful skill in short-hand writing being referred to, I remarked that he (Ewing) " seemed to think that Mr. Stephens was mistaken as to the familiarity of Georgia boys of fourteen with the Declaration of Independence and the Constitution of the United States."

"It was remarkable," Mr. Ewing replied ; "but I have no doubt that Stephens told the truth. Such things run in streaks, in schools, in neighborhoods. A certain set of boys sometimes astonish people by their familiarity with subjects which no one would suppose them to have any knowledge of. One clever and ambitious boy, who is passionately devoted to some particular study, will inspire many of his schoolfellows with a like enthusiasm, and they will make that study a hobby. That was probably the case in Stephens's set ; but I do not suppose that in general the boys of Georgia are any more familiar with the Declaration of Independence and the Constitution of the United States than are the boys of Ohio or any other State."

It will be seen further on, that Calhoun's account of the education of boys in South Carolina was somewhat out of joint with Mr. Stephens's statement as to the mental acquisitions of boys in Georgia.

CHAPTER III.

John C. Calhoun.

I. Notions of Calhoun in the North.—My feelings towards . him.—His personal appearance.—My change of feeling in his favor.

Forty years ago (1848) John C. Calhoun, of South Carolina, was one of the most noted men on the American continent. The rabid abolitionists of the North—of whom I was one—who hated slavery and slaveholders with virulent animosity, felt towards Calhoun the same as Southern men, who hated abolitionists with equal virulence, felt towards William Lloyd Garrison. All through the North, Calhoun was known as the " Great Secessionist," the " Great Nullifier," the " Great Disunionist," and the " Great " bad man generally, who had long

been trying to destroy the Union. As I was
full to the brim of abolition bigotry and preju-
dice, when I went to Washington I was
naturally eager to get a sight of the great
South Carolina nullifier and disunionist; and
when he was pointed out to me, in the Senate
Chamber, I gave him a searching scrutiny.
His appearance satisfied me completely. He
seemed to be a perfect image and embodiment
of the devil. Had I come across his likeness
in a copy of Milton's Paradise Lost, I should
have at once accepted it as a picture of Satan,
and as a masterpiece of some great artist who
had a peculiar genius for Satanic portraiture.
He was tall and gaunt. His complexion was
dark and Indian like, and there seemed to be
an inner complexion of a dark soul shining out
through the skin of the face. His eyes were
large, black, piercing, scintillant. His hair
was iron gray, and rising nearly straight from
the scalp, fell over on all sides, and hung down
in thick masses like a lion's mane. His feat-

ures were strongly marked, and their expression
was firm, stern, aggressive, threatening.

It was some time before I heard Calhoun's
voice, as he seldom addressed the Senate. But
at last a petition from the inhabitants of New
Mexico (one of the Territories recently acquired
from Mexico by our Government) was presented
to the Senate, by Colonel Benton and Senator
Clayton, of Delaware, in which the petitioners
prayed that Congress would protect them
against the introduction of slavery into that
Territory. Here was that everlasting Wilmot
Proviso again, coming up from an unexpected
quarter. It brought Calhoun to his feet, and
his rising at once brought the previously scat-
tered and indifferent attention of the Senate to
a focus. Silence reigned, and every eye was
turned upon the Senator from South Carolina.
He denounced the petition—coming, as he said,
" from a people conquered by our arms "—as
impertinent and insolent, and as an insult to
the Senate and the country. I was much

impressed by the clearness of Calhoun's views, by the bell-like sweetness and resonance of his voice, the elegance of his diction, and the exquisite courtesy of his demeanor. Such a combination of attractive qualities was a revelation to me, and I spontaneously wished that Calhoun was an abolitionist, so we could have him talking on our side. I thought that if he only were on our side, he might even eclipse ·Wendell Phillips as an anti-slavery orator.

The petition from the inhabitants of New Mexico had been prepared at the instigation of Colonel Benton, on purpose to uncover the designs of the slavery extensionists. In fact, it was surmised that Benton wrote the petition himself; and when Calhoun declared that it was an insult to the Senate and the country, and stigmatized it as impertinent and insolent, Benton, who hated Calhoun, was enraged and replied to him with great bitterness. Benton's manner was, and evidently was intended to be, insulting and exasperating. It

seemed to me that Calhoun would be unable to
refrain from resenting it in an emphatic way.
But he treated it with absolute indifference. I
watched him as closely as I could, and it was
impossible to tell from his manner that he was
conscious of anything which Benton was saying.
The debate became general and a good deal of
bad temper was shown. Benton repeatedly
assailed Calhoun in an exasperating fashion, but
he did not seem to mind it. He replied to
several of Benton's attacks, and occasionally
warmed into vehemence, but maintained his
dignified demeanor and exquisite courtesy to
the end of the debate. At the beginning of the
contest, my feelings were against Calhoun and
I wanted him to be worsted; but at the close,
although I was opposed to the principles which
he advocated, my personal feelings were in his
favor, and his physiognomy seemed to have
undergone a change. Instead of looking like a
devil, he impressed me as a high-toned, elegant
gentleman, with a brilliant intellect, a sweet

disposition, a sound heart, and a conscientious devotion to what he believed to be right. I was vexed and astonished at myself that such a change should have occurred in my feelings towards the Great Nullifier. It seemed to me that I was becoming a traitor to my status as an abolitionist ; but as time went on the change also went on in spite of all that I could do.

II. A New Year's Call—The State Rights Doctrine from Calhoun's Lips.

On New Year's day, 1849, I called on Mr. Calhoun, at his request, to explain to him the new system of phonographic writing, which was then exciting a good deal of interest. Mr. Calhoun being too unwell to make or receive calls that day, he utilized the time by taking a lesson in phonography. Accompanied by Master Murphy, I went to Mr. Calhoun's residence at twelve o'clock and stayed till sundown. He was not at all well; in fact, was never again well, and died in fifteen months from that day.

After getting through with phonography, in the
philosophy of which he took great interest, as
he also did in the exhibition of remarkable skill
in its use which was given by Master Murphy,
he branched off into reporting generally, and
said, among other things, that reporters habit-
ually made one mistake in their reports of his
speeches which annoyed him.

" What is that mistake ?" I asked, to which
he replied :

" They make me say ' this *Nation*,' instead
of ' this *Union*.' I never use the word *Nation*
in speaking of the United States ; I always use
the word *Union*, or Confederacy. We are not
a nation, but a *Union*, a confederacy of equal
and sovereign States. England is a nation,
Austria is a nation, Russia is a nation, but the
United States are not a nation."

Then he launched out into his reasons for
never calling the United States a nation, and
touched upon his whole political philosophy. I
was so charmed with his manner, with the

clearness of his ideas and the precision with which he expressed them, that on subsequent occasions I asked him many questions on the subject, which he always copiously answered, and seemingly with pleasure. He used the words sovereign and sovereignty so often in speaking of the "sovereign States" and the "sovereignty of the people," that on one occasion I asked him where sovereignty originated, and how one State got to be more sovereign than the United States—than all the States taken together.

His reply, which follows, I wrote out in short-hand as soon as I could. It is not probable that I reproduced it verbatim, but the substance is accurately given. He said :

"That question goes deep. Sovereignty resides in the people. It is not *created by* them ; it is *born in* them, and cannot be alienated from them. In considering the nature of our institutions, a distinction must be made between sovereignty and government. Government, unlike inborn sovereignty, is a creation of the people—is the instrument devised by the people for exercising their sovereignty over their own affairs and for their own convenience and benefit. Sovereignty is natural, government is artificial. Sovereignty is primary, government is secondary. Sovereignty is inalienable and unchangeable, while government is alienable, and may be changed, or transferred even, at the will of sovereignty—that is to say, at the will of the citizens of the State who are the sovereigns.

"In our Union, or Confederacy, each State is a sovereign State. The thirteen original sovereign States learned by experience that their political necessities comprised two distinct classes of governmental wants; first, local wants pertaining to domestic affairs and circumscribed by State lines ; second, general wants relating to affairs originating or extending beyond State lines. For this reason it became expedient that, in addition to their State governments, which could administer all local affairs, the States should institute a general government, or common agent, to attend to general and common and foreign affairs, such as are common to all the States and require the exercise of jurisdiction beyond State lines. The States did institute such common agent or general government, to wit : the Federal Government, to transact certain business for them ; but they did not endow it with an atom of sovereign power, and in fact could not do so, because sovereignty is inalienable, and perpetually resides, where its Creator originally placed it, in the hearts and minds of individual freemen."

"How then," I asked, "does a State get to be sovereign ?" to which Mr. Calhoun replied :

"The people of a State are a political unit ; as their interests are unified, homogeneous, *one,* they (the people) are combined and solidified into what is simply a larger individuality, and their individual sovereignty is transferred into a unified political or State sovereignty, making the State itself sovereign *within its own lines;* but its sovereignty cannot be extended beyond its own boundaries. The problem which the framers of the Federal Constitution, in their efforts to institute a common agent to act as the servant of the sovereign States, had to solve, was, how to create a government which would answer the purpose of the States without impairing their sovereignty ; in other words, how to secure the services of an efficient servant, and at the same time impose such conditions that their servant would not and could not become their master. Hence, in the Federal Compact or Constitution, they carefully defined and limited the powers which they conferred upon or delegated to their common agent and expressly reserved to themselves all powers not specifically delegated ; and no power can be exercised by their common agent, the Federal Government, unless it is specifically granted in the Federal Compact, which gives it all the power it has. Therefore, if this common agent, the Federal Government, goes beyond the scope of its agreement with its employers (the sovereign States), its action is not binding upon its employers, but is void, and may be repealed or nullified by them. In fact, the compact is broken by such usurpation on the part of the common agent, and any State which, in its own judgment, is injured or oppressed by such unconstitutional action, may, at its own will and pleasure, recede from the original compact or agreement, and secede from the Union."

Here we have stated in an off hand, colloquial way, the famous State Rights or Secession doctrine, which led to our late war, and cost many lives and much money.

III. The Secession Doctrine originally not a South Carolina, but a Massachusetts heresy.

The popular notion is that the State Rights, Secession, or Disunion doctrine was originated by Calhoun and was a South Carolina heresy.

But that popular notion is wrong. According to the best information I have been able to acquire on the subject, the State Rights or Secession doctrine, was originated by Josiah Quincy, and was a Massachusetts heresy.

In 1811, a bill for the admission of what was then called the Orleans Territory (now the State of Louisiana) into the Union as a State, was under discussion in the House of Representatives. Josiah Quincy, of Massachusetts, and many of his colleagues, opposed the measure on the ground that Congress hadn't the constitutional power to admit into the Union a foreign people or State, whose territory was not a part of the original national domain at the time the Constitution was adopted, and the formation of the Union consummated. Mr. Quincy declared that if the bill was passed, and Orleans (now Louisiana) were admitted, the act would be subversive of the Union, and the several States would be freed from their federal bonds and obligations, "and that, as it will be the right of all, [the States,] so it will be the duty of some, to prepare definitely for a separation—amicably if they can, violently if they must."

Mr. Poindexter, with many others, was so shocked by this declaration that he called Mr. Quincy to order; "and," as the report says, (see Abridged Congressional Debates, Vol. IV, page 327,) " Mr. Quincy repeated and justified the remark he had made, which, to save all misapprehension, he committed to writing in the following words : 'If this bill passes, it is my deliberate opinion that it is virtually a dissolution of the Union ; that it will free the States from their moral obligation, and as it will be the right of all, so it will be the duty of some, definitely to prepare for a separation, amicably if they can, violently if they must.' "

The Speaker, Joseph B. Varnum, of Massachusetts, ruled that the last clause of Mr. Quincy's remarks was unparliamentary and out of order. Mr. Quincy appealed from the

Speaker's decision, and his appeal was sustained by a vote of 56 to 53. Thus it was decided by the House of Representatives, under the lead of one of the most enlightened and patriotic sons of Massachusetts, that it was parliamentary and proper to discuss the dissolution of the Union, and to maintain that in case of a certain specified contingency it would be the right of all the States, and the duty of some of them, definitely to prepare for a separation, amicably if they could, violently if they must. Is not this the complete and exact logical sum and outcome of Calhoun's theory, as just given?

The extraordinary scene in which Mr. Quincy thus played the leading *rôle*, occurred in the House of Representatives on the 14th day of January, 1811. Calhoun did not take his seat in that House until the 4th day of the ensuing November. He was then twenty-nine years old. What his convictions were at that time as to the right of secession we have a brief but significant indication. On the 26th day of Novem-

ber, 1811, when war with Great Britain was
becoming imminent, Calhoun submitted to the
House of Representatives a report on Foreign
Relations, in which occurred the following
memorable passage, two words of which I shall
take the liberty of italicising :

" If we have not rushed to the field of battle
like the nations who are led by the mad ambition of a single chief or the avarice of a
corrupted court, it has not proceeded from a
fear of war, but from our love of justice and
humanity. That proud spirit of liberty and
independence, which sustained our fathers in
the successful assertion of their liberties against
foreign aggression, is not yet sunk. The patriotic fire of the Revolution still burns in the
American breast with a holy inextinguishable
flame, and will conduct *this nation* to those
high destinies, which are not less the reward of
dignified moderation, than of exalted valor."

This passage was widely published at the
time, and deservedly gave great prestige to Cal-

houn's name ; but the present reader (if he be
an observing one) will probably be most struck
by the fact that in it Calhoun, with his own
hand (and not by means of a mistaken reporter's hand), wrote "this nation" instead of
"this Union." It is evident, therefore, that he
had not then adopted the disunion or secession
doctrines which had been broached in the House
of Representatives ten months before, by Josiah
Quincy, of Massachusetts.

Two years afterwards, on January 8th, 1813,
(see page 656 of the same Volume of Debates.)
Henry Clay taunted Quincy and his associates
with their "plot to dismember the Union," and,
referring to Quincy's declaration, made two
years before, exclaimed : "The gentleman cannot have forgotten his own sentiment, uttered
even on the floor of this House, ' Peaceably if
we can, forcibly if we must !'"

Thirty-three years after Josiah Quincy had
thus taken the lead in advocating the doctrine
of disunion and secession, to wit, in 1844, when

the question of the annexation of Texas was
agitating the country, another distinguished son
of Massachusetts, Charles Francis Adams, then
a member of the Massachusetts Legislature,
followed up Mr. Quincy's lead, by introducing
a resolution embodying the doctrine so long
before initiated by Mr. Quincy in the House of
Representatives.   Mr.   Adams's   resolution
declared in almost the same words that had
been used by Mr. Quincy in the debate on the
admission of Louisiana, that the General Government has not the constitutional power to
unite an independent foreign state with the
United States, as no such power had been delegated to it, and that " the Commonwealth of
Massachusetts, faithful to the compact between
the people of the United States, according to
the plain meaning and intent in which it was
understood and acceded to by them, is sincerely
anxious for its preservation, and that it is determined, as it doubts not other States are, to
submit to undelegated Powers in no body of

men on earth; and that the project of the annexation of Texas, unless resisted on the threshold, may tend to drive these States into a dissolution of the Union."

Calhoun could not ask for any better doctrine of disunion and secession than was presented in that resolution, and that resolution was adopted by the Legislature of Massachusetts, under the lead of Charles Francis Adams who, four years afterwards, was the Free-soil candidate for the Vice-Presidency of that Union whose possible dissolution he so calmly contemplated in 1844. I do not present these facts for the purpose of making out a condemnatory case against Massachusetts. That magnificent old Commonwealth can stand the truth; and so can her illustrious sons. The truth is that in times of wild excitement, when we were all running at the eyes and nose with political influenza and frothing at the mouth with sectional madness, it was customary for all sorts of people to talk glibly about disunion, and about "letting the South go." Even Charles Sumner said : "If they will only go, we will build a bridge of gold for them to go over on." We didn't know how dear to our hearts the Union was until it was assailed by hostile arms, and we were in immediate danger of losing it.

It is possible that Calhoun's adulatory admirers will not thank me for defending him against what they may consider one of his strongest claims upon their admiration ; but it is due to the spirit of justice and fair play that the truth of this matter should be presented. Ever since I can remember anything about public affairs, Calhoun has been anathematised and vituperated with venomous animosity as the one man, the only man responsible for the prevalence of disunion and secession doctrines. I zealously joined in the outcry against him for years, and hated his very name, until I became acquainted with him and with the facts. I have no intention now of attempting to exonerate him from the responsibilities which he incurred by his political course, but I do wish to treat him fairly. And for that purpose I wish fairly to apportion the responsibility for the original insemination of the public mind with the doctrines of disunion and secession ; and without intending disrespect to any State or any statesmen by the application of an old adage to the case, I insist that what is sauce for the South Carolina goose is also sauce for the Massachusett's gander.

Inasmuch as the doctrines of disunion and secession have became obsolete, and the course of events has determined that we are a Nation. and a Nation with a big N, I will not give Webster's refutation of the doctrines, but will dismiss the subject with a simple recurrence to the remark which introduced it, namely : Calhoun's declaration that it annoyed him to have reporters represent him as calling the United States a Nation instead of a Union. After the exposition which has been given of the great South Carolinian's views, the reader will readily understand why such a misrepresentation of his language was so annoying to Calhoun.

IV. Calhoun's Views on the Education of Boys—His Opinion of General Jackson.

During the interview on New Year's Day, 1849, the value of phonography as an educational instrument came under discussion, and Calhoun branched off into educational methods generally. He contrasted Southern with Northern education, and thought that the people of the North were fundamentally wrong as to their notions on the subject. He said they cultivated the intellect almost exclusively, to the neglect of everything else, and especially to the neglect of the body. It will be seen from Calhoun's account of the training of South Carolina boys that it differed somewhat from the training of Georgia boys, according to the statement of Alexander H. Stephens, given at the close of the preceding chapter.

"Look at that boy," he said, nodding

towards Master Murphy, who was small in stature, but had a large and finely developed head, and a countenance indicating unusual intellectual culture in one so young :—" Look at that boy, with the body of a child and the head of a man. He looks as intellectual as a college professor, and yet see how deficient he is in strength and physical toughness. In South Carolina, instead of pushing a boy of his age in his studies, we would have him riding horses, leaping fences and shooting squirrels. We would build up his body before we set his brain at work. As soon as he became robust and hardy, his head could take care of itself. A people who train their children and youth, generation after generation, as that boy has been trained, may become brilliant in intellectual development and profound in the learning of the schools, but they will lose their grip on matters of public and practical importance and have to take an inferior position as to great questions and great affairs."

The South Carolina method of educating boys, as it was set forth by Calhoun, reminds one of the old Persian custom of teaching their youth " to ride on horseback, shoot arrows, and speak the truth."

In the light of subsequent events, I have sometimes wondered, if Calhoun had lived fifteen years longer, if he would still have believed that the North was running to seed through excessive intellectual culture, while the South, owing to what he considered its better methods of education, was getting a firmer and more tenacious grip on public and important practical matters, and so gravitating to a *superior* "position as to great questions and great affairs."

A little while before the interview terminated, I asked Mr. Calhoun what kind of a man General Jackson was.   The effect of the question upon him made a profound impression upon me.   Had I not been so young and inexperienced, I would not—I could not have asked

him such a question. It did not occur to me
that he and Jackson had been inexpressibly
bitter and relentless foes for many years. As
soon as the question was put, Calhoun sank
into profound quiescence, seemed to be unconscious of my presence, and was apparently
absorbed in introspective memories. Then his
relations to Jackson flashed vividly into my
·mind; I was appalled at my blunder, and
awaited the result with trepidation. Calhoun's
revery continued but a short time. Soon he
looked at me benignantly, and said :

"General Jackson was a great man."

The surpassingly beautiful expression of Calhoun's luminous eyes and the sweet, gentle tone
of his voice, as he thus answered my question,
are now present with me, as I write, although
that answer was given more than forty years
ago. It seemed as though, in his brief, absorb-
ing revery, he had reviewed and passed judgment upon his relations with General Jackson.
The general was in his grave, and he was him-

self beginning to be enveloped with the shadow
of death.   Why should he, a dying man, continue to hate him who was already dead ?   He
would not continue to hate him.   It seemed as
though this, or something equivalent to it,
passed through Calhoun's mind, and touched
the inmost nobility of his nature, and caused
him to give the answer which came from him
like a renunciation of all his animosity and an
assertion of spiritual reconciliation with his dead
foe.

V. Calhoun's Quarrel with General Jackson, and its result.

As I became better acquainted with Calhoun,
I liked him better.   At last, I had a genuine
affection for him, and mourned over what
seemed to me to have been his political deca-
dence ; and I have mourned over it to this hour.
No young man on this continent ever started on
a public career with brighter, nobler promise
than did that gifted, pure-souled young South

Carolinian. He was born in 1782—the same year in which Benton, Webster, Martin Van Buren and General Cass were born—Clay being five years his senior. He entered Congress in 1811 and immediately rose to distinction. He had a convincing and attractive way of expressing his ideas with both tongue and pen.

The paragraph I have given from his report on Foreign Relations shows what a captivating style he had. Whatever he did or said was popular. During the war of 1812, and down to the period of his Vice-Presidency in Jackson's first term (1829), Calhoun's course was patriotic, brilliant and beneficent. He was as popular in the North as in the South. He was an especial favorite in New England ; a fact which seems strange to us now. He was elected Vice-President in 1824, when no other candidate was elected by the people ; the contest for the Presidency being thrown into the House of Representatives, and resulting in the election of John Quincy Adams. After Calhoun's re-election as

Vice President, on the Jackson ticket, in 1828, he was in the direct line of the Democratic succession to the Presidency. But there came a fatal quarrel between him and Old Hickory Jackson, and all chance of his further national preferment was immediately and forever blighted. The cause of this quarrel was the disclosure of the fact that in 1819 Calhoun, while Secretary of War in Monroe's first Administration, had filed an opinion condemning Jackson's course in Florida.

It will be remembered that at that time Florida was owned by Spain; that the Spaniards incited the Indians to murder the American settlers in Alabama and Georgia, and that there were British emissaries helping the Spaniards in this nefarious work; that Jackson, then a major-general in the United States army and commander of the Southern division of it, was sent to the scene of the outrages to pacificate affairs and protect his countrymen, and with the understanding that, although the

Government did not wish to appear before the world as countenancing extreme measures, it would wink at any means of pacification to which the commanding general should find it necessary to resort; that General Jackson, on arriving at the theatre of operations and finding an outrageous state of affairs, began the work of " pacification " with his accustomed energy, hung two British emissaries—Arbuthnot and Ambrister—stormed some of the Spanish fortifications, and soon brought a state of Jacksonian peace and safety to pass. Jackson's proceedings of course excited the wrath of the British and the Spaniards, and threatened to involve the United States in war with both Spain and Great Britain. His conduct was severely censured in Congress, and it was made to appear that he had acted without any warrant whatever from the Government for his violent course. This injustice aroused the old warrior to ungovernable fury. and he threatened to go to Washington and cut off the ears of Congressmen who

maligned him.   The Administration was called
upon to discipline the belligerent general, and
President Monroe asked for written opinions on
the case from the members of his Cabinet.
The opinions were handed in, and all of them,
except Calhoun's, were in Jackson's favor.

Those Cabinet opinions were under the seal
of official secrecy, and nobody outside of the
Administration knew what they were.   But
Jackson in some way got the idea firmly fixed
in his mind that Calhoun was the member of
the Cabinet who took the lead in defending him
on that critical occasion.   That made Jackson
Calhoun's devoted friend, and caused him to do
everything he could to secure his advancement.
It may be imagined, therefore, what a shock
the disclosure of the truth was to Old Hickory,
and with what rage it filled him.   He immediately cast off Calhoun as a traitor and hypocrite, and swore everlasting vengeance against
him.

How this disclosure, which was so disastrous

to Calhoun, happened to be made, nobody
seems to know with absolute certainty. Different explanations of it, some of them very
elaborate, have been published. When 1 first
went to Washington, in 1848, the matter was
still a topic for gossip and discussion, and there
were hundreds of people who had gone through
the excitement and turmoil it occasioned, and
supposed they knew all about it. The general
run of gossip on the subject was that if the
Peggy O'Neil scandal and controversy had not
occurred, the Calhoun disclosure would not
have been made. Peggy O'Neil was the handsome daughter of a Washington tavern-keeper,
who married Purser Timberlake of the United
States navy. Timberlake died, and his widow
was wooed and won by General John H. Eaton,
of Tennessee, who was Jackson's intimate
friend, and was appointed Secretary of War in
Jackson's first Cabinet. And thus Peggy O'Neil
blossomed out into "a Cabinet lady," and was
eligible to the highest society in Washington.

Unfortunately, there had been derogatory rumors about her while she was Mrs. Timberlake. Her husband was absent at sea for many months, and she, being attractive and full of "the spirit of society," received a good deal of attention from officers of the army and navy. She was talked about in an unpleasant way, and had to pay the penalty which is exacted from every handsome woman who accepts too much homage from other women's husbands while her own husband is absent.

Gossip became still more rife and acrimonious when General Eaton married the widow Timberlake ; and when, by his becoming Secretary of War, she became "a Cabinet lady," the wives of other members of the Cabinet felt that a blow had been struck at the honor and prestige of their sacred society circle. They met the impending calamity with Spartan resolution. They announced that they would have no social relations whatever with Mrs. Eaton née O'Neil. They would not receive calls from her ; they

would not make calls on her ; they would not
grace with their presence any social entertain-
ment which she was permitted to attend. As
they were upheld by their lady friends, Mrs.
Eaton was in effect excluded from society.
The action of the Cabinet ladies was a social
thunder-clap. It occasioned a prodigious sensa-
tion. General Jackson was frantic with indignation and rage at the insult to the wife of his
bosom friend, General Eaton, and swore, by
the Eternal, that she should be received by the
other Cabinet ladies. The contention convulsed
society. As the contest went on, it became
apparent that for once Old Hickory had found
his match. He had conquered the British and
the Spaniards and numberless Indian tribes,
but he could not conquer one little tribe of
white women. He was worsted in the fight,
and other annoying complications being drawn
into the social and political swirl, the Cabinet
was re-organized, General Eaton going out of

office, and Mrs. Eaton going out of public
notice.

It happened that the husbands of the ladies
who organized this social war were all particular
friends to Calhoun. They were in fact known
as "The Calhoun members of the Cabinet."
General Jackson, animated by his gratitude for
Calhoun's supposed loyalty to him when his
enemies were seeking to destroy him in 1819,
had generously given three of the Vice-President's partisans places in the Cabinet; and it
was the wives of those three Cabinet officers
who instigated the crusade against the wife of
the President's friend. And it was said that it
was to punish Calhoun, and his set, that his
opinion, hostile to Jackson, was unearthed and
brought to light. I had several conversations
on the subject with a son of one of the Calhoun
Cabinet officers. He had heard his father and
mother and their friends discuss the matter a
myriad times. They cherished an absolute conviction that the divulgation of Calhoun's opinion

was purposely made by the friends of General Eaton to avenge Mrs. Eaton's wrongs. But this belief was not universal. Many saw a political manœuvre in the disclosure, and charged it upon Calhoun's political rivals. Van Buren's enemies saw his cunning hand in it; Calhoun believed that Van Buren was the author of the disclosure; and color was lent to his belief by the fact that Van Buren was the chief gainer by the rupture between the President and Vice-President. He displaced Calhoun in the line of political succession, and fell heir to the Presidency, which, previous to the rupture, was coming straight to Calhoun. This led to a lifelong estrangement between those two distinguished Democrats; and their estrangement led to the rejection of Van Buren as a Presidential candidate by the Democratic Convention in 1844, and to his acceptance of the Free-soil nomination, and the consequent defeat of General Cass, in 1848, as narrated in our first chapter. William H. Crawford, of Georgia, was also charged with the disclosure of Calhoun's opinion, and so were others ; but the popular belief ascribed it to the retaliatory vengeance of Mrs. Eaton's friends.

It is possible that the convulsions of the Mrs. Eaton war indirectly helped to erupt the Calhoun opinion from the secret archives of the Cabinet, but thus far no absolute proof of the precise way in which it was divulged has been made public. But divulged it was, and the effect upon Calhoun's political career was calamitous. He was estranged from the dominant members of the Democratic party, and as he had no affinities for the Whigs, his only resource was to develop a party of his own ; and that he at once set about doing. How he did it, and what terrible results came of it, are matters of general history.

In order to carry out his determination Calhoun had to bring about a fundamental change in the opinion of the South as to slavery. Up to that time it was generally conceded that slavery was a moral and political evil, a vast, ineradicable national cancer which the country must bear and suffer under as best it might. Calhoun set at work to " correct this erroneous notion," and, so far as the South was concerned, he accomplished his purpose. In a powerful speech which he made in the Senate in 1837, on resolutions with regard to slavery introduced by himself, he said :

" This agitation has produced one happy effect, at least—it has compelled us of the South to look into the nature and character of this great institution, [slavery,] and to correct many false impressions that even we had entertained in relation to it. Many in the South once believed that it was a moral and political evil. *That folly and delusion are gone.* We see it now in its true light, and regard it as the most safe and stable basis for free institutions in the world. It is impossible with us that the conflict can take place between labor and capital, which makes it so difficult to establish and maintain free institutions in all wealthy and highly civilized nations, where such institutions as ours do not exist. The Southern States are an aggregate, in fact, of communities, not of individuals. Every plantation is a little community, with the master at its head, who concentrates in himself the united interest of capital and labor, of which he is the common representative. The small communities aggregated make the State in all, whose action, labor, and capital is equally represented and perfectly harmonised."

In the course of this speech, Calhoun said that "a mysterious Providence had brought together two races, from different portions of the globe, and placed them together in nearly equal numbers in the Southern portion of this Union ;" to which Clay replied that "to call a generation of slave-trading pirates (who brought the negroes to this country) 'a mysterious Providence,' was an insult to the Supreme Being." Clay's reply was admired, but it did not lessen the influence of Calhoun's speech in the South.

VI. Calhoun's Fascination in Personal Intercourse.

After that New Year's day, 1849, I occasionally met Mr. Calhoun, and every time I had an opportunity to hear him converse and to study his character, my appreciation of him was strengthened. He was by all odds the most fascinating man in private intercourse that I ever met. His conversational powers were marvelous. His voice was clear, sweet and mellow, with a musical, metallic ring in it which gave it strength without diminishing its sweetness. His pronunciation and enunciation were perfect. His manner was simple and unpretentious. He talked on the most abstruse subjects with the guileless simplicity of a prattling child. His ideas were so clear and his language so plain that he made a path of light through any subject he discussed.

Harriet Martineau said, a dozen or fifteen years before the period (1849) of which I am writing, that " Calhoun's mind had lost the power of communicating with other minds." I can understand how a stranger might get that impression of Calhoun. There were at least two Calhouns, perhaps there were several. That is to say, his ideas and sentiments on different subjects were so differentiated, so sharply defined, and so rigidly separated from one another, that the man himself seemed to be a different personage at different times, according to the question or subject before him. His faculties were not compacted into a mental or psychological nation ; they were simply a confederacy, and every one of them was a sovereign faculty, which could think and act for itself, independently of all the rest. His convictions on the subject of slavery were as fixed and unchangeable as an elementary principle of nature ; and, as to them, his mind was incapable of exchanging ideas with other minds. That portion of his mind was a hermit, and it led a hermit's existence ; and if Miss Martineau attempted to intrude into that hermit's cell, she found it impossible to communicate with its occupant.

Calhoun's kindness of heart was inexhaustible. He impressed me as being deeply but unobtrusively religious, and was so morally clean and spiritually pure that it was a pleasure to have one's soul get close to his soul—a feeling that I never had for any other man. He seemed to exhale an atmosphere of purity, as fresh and sweet and bracing as a breeze from the prairie, the ocean, or the mountain—an atmosphere which one could safely breathe all in and be better and purer from the inspiration. He was inexpressibly urbane, refined, gentle, winning; and yet he was strong and thoroughly manly, with an elegant and engaging invincibleness pervading his softness and gentleness. I admired Benton; I admired Clay still more; I admired Webster, on the intellectual side, most of all; but I loved Calhoun; and as I came to know him well, and saw his exquisitely beautiful nature mirrored in his face, his countenance no longer seemed Satanic, but angelic, and his benignant greeting in the morning was like a benediction that lasted the whole day.

It is believed that Calhoun's political life was so embittered that he got no comfort out of it, and that it grew less and less satisfactory as he drew near its end ; but in private and social relations he was blessed with strongest and most disinterested friendships, and his last days were enriched and sweetened by

> " That best portion of a good man's life,
> His little, nameless, unremembered acts
> Of kindness and of love."

My acquaintance, at the age when my character was in process of development and formation, with John C. Calhoun and Jefferson Davis was of incomputable benefit to me. The fact that of all the distinguished men I saw in Washington, the two whose political course was the most obnoxious to me were the very two whom I most liked personally, had then and afterwards a powerful effect upon my mind, my heart and my life. And this effect was deepened by the fact that some of those with whose political principles I most keenly sympathized were the ones whose personal characters were the most distasteful to me. The struggles of mind and the travail of spirit which the conflicting thoughts and emotions consequent upon such a state of things occasioned in me, caused me to be born again as to my notions of public men and public affairs. I learned to distinguish between a man's political principles and his personal character, and there was developed in me a disposition to extend to the convictions and conduct of others the same forbearance and charity which every man likes to have accorded to his own conduct and convictions.

CHAPTER IV.

Thomas H. Benton.

I. Benton's hatred of Calhoun.—The Great South Carolinian and the Great Missourian contrasted.

Notwithstanding Calhoun's lovable character, he had at least one bitter and relentless foe —Thomas H. Benton, of Missouri. Benton was called the Great Missourian ; Calhoun, the Great South Carolinian ; and their natures differed more and were more widely sundered than their respective States. Indeed, it would be difficult to find two other co-temporary Americans, of equal distinction, so absolutely contrasted in body, mind, principles, tastes and manners as were Benton and Calhoun. Calhoun was slender and delicate of frame; Benton was massive and muscular. Calhoun was speculative, theoretical and philosophical ; Benton was matter of-fact, statistical and practical. Calhoun was sympathetic, sensitive and considerate ; Benton was cold, hard and ruthless. To rub Calhoun's nature against Benton's was like rubbing the tender skin of an infant against the corrugated hide of a rhinocerous. And then Calhoun sought to destroy the Union, while Benton was a fierce upholder of the Union. Previous to his discovery of Calhoun's ultimate motives in forcing the doctrines of State Rights and the right of secession upon the attention of the South, Benton was his friend and coädjutor, but as soon as he made that discovery he began to dislike him, and when he became convinced that Calhoun would be glad to have the Union destroyed, he made open war upon him ; and from that time the Great Missourian hated the Great South Carolinian with rancorous and unappeasable hatred.

II. How to Estimate Character.

In estimating a man's character, and in passing judgment upon his conduct, we should keep in mind what the psychologists and biologists call his heredity and his environment. According to the doctrine on this subject, a man's heredity, or inborn nature, comes to him through his parents, from his entire line of ancestry, and is set in him beyond the power of elementary change. The *elements* of character that are born in him may be developed or withered, but they can not be changed any more than the functions of his senses can be changed. The sense of seeing cannot be changed into the sense of hearing, nor can the passion for destroying be changed into the sentiment of benevolence. Either of these elementary traits may be strengthened by cultivation or weakened by neglect, but it cannot be *changed* into anything else. The sum of one's character will depend on the relative development, neglect or suppression of its inborn elements ; and his environment—which is the sum of all the influences which act upon his heredity—is the medium through which and by which the development, neglect, or suppression of the inborn elements is brought to pass.

A tragic incident which occurred thirty-five years ago in a remote section of what is now West Virginia, may help persons who are not familiar with the theory of heredity and environment, to get some notion of it. A family named Russell undertook to domesticate a young bear and to change its carnivorous heredity into a herbivorous proclivity. Mr. Russell was an advocate of vegetarianism. He believed that most of the evils of human nature come of eating too much meat. He imagined that the ferocity of the carnivori was owing to their habitual flesh diet, and that it might be extinguished by a prolonged course of vegetarian discipline. Having caught an unweaned bear cub, he determined to demonstrate the correctness of his theory. So the creature was fed on milk, sweet corn, pumpkins, berries, and fruits of all kinds. It was not permitted to have any meat. It grew rapidly, and was so playful and amiable it seemed as though Mr. Russell's theory was going to be demonstrated beyond all cavil. It was the custom, when evening approached, to chain the bear to a post on the lawn, lest it should wander off in the night. One evening, Mr. Russell's eldest boy, a fine lad of fifteen years, who had been hunting, came home with a string of birds and squirrels that he had shot. In passing the bear's post, the boy stopped to have a little play. The bear, smelling the blood of the birds and squirrels, attempted to seize them with his teeth ; whereupon the boy struck him over the nose with the string of game. This awakened the animal's sleeping heredity ; and springing upon the boy he began to devour him before the eyes of his mother, who stood on the piazza and shrieked for help. Mr. Russell and several field hands hearing her cries, rushed to the spot. but they were too late to save the boy. The bear was immediately killed ; and thus ended the attempt to change the heredity of a carnivorous beast to the traits of a herbivorous animal, by means of a vegetarian environment.

This doctrine of heredity and environment, when rightly understood, explains many social phenomena which, without its aid, are incomprehensible. For example, a man who for years has been trusted by a whole community —who has been the faithful executor of many wills and the faithful guardian of many orphans—suddenly runs away with the funds entrusted to his care, and everybody is aghast at the unaccountable occurrence. How could such a thing have happened ? is the universal exclamation. It could happen just as that vegetarian bear could so unexpectedly devour that boy. The carnivorous appetite was hereditary in the bear and manifested itself the moment it received sufficient provocation. So,

too, the thieving, robbing, defrauding proclivity
was hereditary in that good man, but was kept
in abeyance by his environment until an over-
mastering opportunity provoked it into action,
and the phenomenally trustworthy man ran
away with the trust money. Any unexpected
outburst of vice or break down of character on
the one hand, or any exhibition of noble traits
which a person was not suspected of possessing
on the other hand, can be readily explained by
the application of this theory. In fact, it
covers the entire range of the development of
human character ; and now let us see how it
works in explaining the personal characteristics
of Colonel Benton.

III. Benton's Character.

Benton's heredity, both as to physique and
mentality, was peculiar and striking. He was
born with characteristics resembling those of
the bear, the bull and the eagle. He was
ferocious, brave, keen-sighted and high-soaring.

In mind, dignity and patriotism he was a Roman Senator of the highest type; and in physique, temper and ferocity he was a Roman gladiator, who somehow had become imbedded in the nineteenth century. He had large bones, which were covered with thick and hard muscles. He was about five feet and ten inches in height, had broad shoulders, a deep chest, large hips and strong limbs. His head, which was of great size, was largest at the base. All the animal propensities, especially those which give cunning and courage, were powerfully developed. His courage was so predominant and combative, that he seldom cared to resort to cunning to compass his ends; but when he did undertake to play Indian, no savage that ever infested the wilderness could cope with him.

His organs of observation were large and active, and his firmness and self-esteem were so prominently developed that his massive head ran up to a peak like the Island of Teneriffe. His countenance was romanesque, with the blended expression of the eagle and the lion. It is doubtful if we ever had a man in public life, in America, equal to Colonel Benton in physical strength, endurance and courage, in toughness and elasticity of constitution, and in mental and moral fortitude. There have been men who equalled, and perhaps excelled him in some of these qualities, but nobody else has exhibited such an admirable combination of them all.

Benton's early training, and in fact the environment of all the first half of his life, was such as would bring all his natural traits to their fullest development. He was born in 1782, in an obscure hamlet in North Carolina. When he was eight years old his father died, and his widowed mother removed to Tennessee. He had little opportunity to go to school, but he studied hard at home in the evening, after the day's duties had been done. Fortunately, his mother was a refined, pious, God-fearing woman, who brought up her fatherless children in the nurture and admonition of the Lord. Benton's religion, though it modified his heredity, could not change it. He was a robust and ferocious Christian—just the kind for his day and generation. As he grew to manhood, he was more or less engaged in fighting Indians and wild beasts and half-wild neighbors. After a time he studied law and entered the slightly more civilized arena of the bar, where foes did not tomahawk and scalp, but only knifed and pistolled one another. In that wild life, the great law of the survival of the fittest was inexorably supreme ; and the fittest, of course, meant the fittest for that kind of life. Benton was one of the fittest. He survived and thrived ; he even survived a desperate personal encounter with Old Hickory Jackson in the streets of Nashville ; and so far as I know he was the only man that ever did survive a personal fight with Old Hickory.

In 1815 Benton went to Missouri, then a Territory, inhabited by a fierce population, where his fights continued, with the usual result. What that result was may be inferred from a declaration he made in the Senate, after a Senator had referred to what he called "a quarrel" of Benton's. "Mr. President, sir," said the Great Missourian sternly, "the Senator is mistaken, sir. I never *quarrel*, sir; but I sometimes fight, sir; and whenever I fight, sir, a funeral follows, sir!"

Missouri was admitted to the Union in 1820, and Benton was at once elected United States Senator from that State, and took his seat in March, 1821. He was re-elected four times in succession, and so served as Senator thirty years continuously, his last term expiring March 3rd, 1851. When he entered the United States Senate, he was within a few days of his fortieth year and his character had been formed and fixed. What that character was, the reader can imagine, if he will recall to mind what Benton's heredity was, and how it had been acted upon and developed by his whole hard, struggling, wild, contentious life. And in passing judgment upon a man's life, we must remember that he is to be judged according to his character and not according to our character, according to the time in which he lived and not according to the time in which we live, and according to the circumstances which environed him and not according to those which surround us.

Benton, as I have said, was a Roman gladiator in body and temper. It was his custom to bathe and scrub down his body to his hips every morning, and from his hips to his feet every afternoon. The implement he used was the roughest kind of a horsehair brush ; and with this his body servant would curry him down with all his might. A friend, who saw the brush, shook his head over it, whereupon Benton grimly said : " Why, sir, if I were to *touch* you with that brush, sir, you would cry murder, sir." On being asked why he thus scrubbed half of his body in the morning and the other half in the afternoon, he replied : " The Roman gladiators did it, sir." Under this treatment,

his skin had become a sheath of leather, devoid
of sensibility, and shutting him out from sympathy with the sensibilities of others. Metaphorically, as well as physically, he was probably the thickest skinned man of his time.
This enabled him to go scathless through
contests from which others would come out
with sorely wounded spirits and bleeding hearts.

IV. Benton's Characteristics as a Debater.

Seemingly, Benton was indifferent alike to
praise or blame. But he was capable of intense
wrath when he thought that any project of his
own, or any public matter in which he took an
interest, was unfairly treated. And when he
was thoroughly roused to anger, he was most
dangerous ; for he never lost his self possession,
and always used his anger as a wrath-power
wherewith to propel his mental machinery. He
spoke with deliberation, and was noted for his
short, emphatic, incisive sentences. He had a
biting wit, and a grim humor, which were

pleasant to everybody except the victims of
them. When he wanted to torture an opponent,
he had a way of elevating his voice into a rasp-
ing squeal of sarcasm which was intolerably
exasperating and sometimes utterly maddening.
The word *sir* was a formidable missile on his
tongue, and he brought it into play with a
frequency which nothing but his powerful utter-
ance and commanding manner prevented from
becoming absurd. He had a way of repeating
a sentence over and over and over, with slight
variations, which was exceedingly effective.

In the debate on the petition from the people
of New Mexico to be protected from the introduction of slavery into that Territory, which I
heretofore said (see page 149) brought Calhoun
to his feet, and the preparation of which was
instigated by Benton, Senator Westcott, of
Florida, in commenting adversely on the petition, read portions of it to illustrate his argument. In thus reading from the petition he
inadvertently read the phrase, "the people of

New Mexico" twice, and omitted the following phrase, by which an erroneous idea of the nature of the petition was given. Benton at once arose, and majestically reaching forth his hand to Westcott, who stood near him, he imperiously said :

" Will you hand me that petition, sir?"

Senator Westcott, taken by surprise, spontaneously handed over the petition. Benton took it, and turning towards Vice President Dallas, who was presiding over the Senate, said :

" Mr. President, sir, I wish to read the words that the Senator from Florida left out. He read it twice, sir, as a petition from the people of New Mexico. He read it twice, sir, as relating to the people of New Mexico, and he read, sir, 'the people of New Mexico' twice—[laughter]— twice, sir, and by reading it twice he thought himself entitled to leave out the few following words." Benton hurled " the people of New Mexico, twice, sir," like a missile at the opponents of the petition. On every repetition of the word "twice" his voice struck a higher key and rang out with increased power; his mighty arm swept through the air with majestic gesticulation, his eyes blazed, his massive form dilated and towered with indignation, and he looked as though he was ready to sink the Senator in the gladiator at the slightest physical provocation.

Benton's peculiar mental formation made him mighty on the plane of physical affairs. He knew the material resources of the country, and everything thereunto appertaining, by heart. He believed in solid, material things, and hated whatever was flimsy or flabby. Speculative projects found no favor with him; to win his support, a scheme had to be sound from end to end and all over substantial.

Benton was not an eloquent speaker, but he was always interesting. His speeches were packed with facts and filled with information. His grim wit and mocking sarcasm gave a pungent relish to his style which was exceedingly agreeable. The indomitable old Indian fighter was usually apparent in his manner ; and metaphorically speaking it was easy to detect the whir of the tomahawk and the gleam of the scalping knife in his acrid sentences. He did not confine himself strictly to the question in debate, but struck out into any by-path of animadversion in which he scented game, looking for scalps in sequestered issues and dealing blows at every head he could find. Sometimes he would ramble on in a discursive way for hours, and make a speech that would fill six. eight, or ten columns of the *Intelligencer ;* and then, after the speech had been written out. he would expunge all the extraneous matter it contained, so it would make only two or three columns in print. The reporters. being paid by the column. did not like his curtailments. I remember, on one occasion, that my report of a portion of one of his speeches made four columns, and he cut it down to a column and a half. It was difficult for an impecunious young reporter to feel friendly towards a great man who was accustomed to behave in such a ruthless manner as that.

V. His Egotism

The most marked trait of Benton's character was his egotism, which was so conspicuous that it could not escape the notice of the most indifferent observer. Egotism is usually offensive and almost invariably excites disgust. But Benton's egotism was so vast, so towering, so part and parcel of the man, that it was not at all offensive, and never excited disgust. On the contrary, it excited admiration and gave the beholder of it pleasure. One could not help feeling that the old ironclad's egotism was a sort of national institution in which every patriotic American could take a just pride ; that his egotism was as proper to him as its apex is to a pyramid ; that, in fact, it had come to pass through a natural and fitting process of evolution, and was simply the harmonious apex of his pyramidal character. Benton's egotism pervaded him utterly, and was apparent in everything which he said or did. It made Benton the centre of the universe to Benton—the central force which moved all things, the central orb around which all other orbs revolved. In his opinion, whatever public matter he had to do with at all, took its shape entirely from his touch, and its success was owing to him exclusively. It is well known that General Jackson, while he was President, destroyed the United States Bank ; and it is universally believed that no man but General Jackson had the nerve to begin an attack upon that "Financial Monster," as the bank was called. Benton, with others, took sides with Jackson against the bank. Years afterwards, when Jackson was dead, a gentleman who was walking with Benton in Washington remarked, as they passed the equestrian statue of the general, that Jackson was a very wonderful man, to which Benton responded :

"Yes, sir ; General Jackson was a great man, sir—a very great man, sir. He was of great use to *me*, sir, in *my* war upon the United States Bank, sir."

When Benton's great work, "Thirty Years in the United States Senate," was about to come from the press, its publishers, (the Appletons,) sent a messenger to him to get his views as to the number of copies that should be printed. The messenger having presented the case, the old man loftily said :

"Sir, they can ascertain from the last census how many persons there are in the United States who can read, sir ;" and that was the only suggestion he would condescend to make. That he believed his book would be read by everybody who could read at all, I have no doubt. He supposed that whatever he said or wrote was eagerly sought for by all sorts of people. An amusing proof of this is given in the very book in question. In an autobiographical sketch which serves as an introduction to the work, Benton, in speaking of his public career, says :

"From that time [the date of Benton's first election to the Senate] his life was in the public eye, and the bare enumeration of the measures of which he was the author and the prime promoter, would be almost a history of Congress Legislation. The enumeration is unnecessary here; the long list is known throughout the length and breadth of the land—repeated with the familiarity of household words from the great cities on the seaboard to the lonely cabins on the frontier—and studied by the little boys who feel an honorable ambition beginning to stir within their bosoms, and a laudable desire to learn something of the history of their country."

Such immeasurable and self-blinding egotism as that fairly takes one's breath away. The idea of the little boys of the country devoting their spare time to the reading of Thomas H. Benton's Congressional speeches, reports and bills, is a conception so transcendently egotistical that one's powers of description and characterization wilt before it. It is not probable that any little boy "from the cities on the seaboard to the lonely cabins on the frontier" ever read a dozen pages of anything which came from Benton's tongue or pen ; nor is it likely that one adult in ten thousand is familiar with his works.

In the autumn of 1870 I was in St. Louis, and embraced the opportunity to talk with some of Benton's old neighbors. They were ready enough to talk about him, and I heard a few anecdotes that were so characteristic of him, that I seemed to hear his voice and see his imperious bearing in them. Many years before, when the Czar Nicholas was the most conspicuous personage in Europe, some one was telling how strangers knelt in his presence. On finishing the narrative the speaker said to Benton :

"I suppose, Colonel, that you would not think of kneeling to the Czar ?" to which he responded, with his most imperial emphasis :

" No, sir ! No, sir ! An American kneels only to God and woman, sir."

In 1856 Benton was running for Governor of Missouri, (he left the Senate in 1851,) against an opponent named Trusten Polk. They canvassed the State, and on one occasion, when Benton stepped forward to speak, he began by saying, in a meditative style :

" T-r-u s-ten Polk ! T-r-u-s-ten Polk ! A man that nobody trusts ; a knave in politics and a hypocrite in religion !"

A few years before, (I think it was in 1852 or '54,) Benton was running for Congress in Missouri. He and his rival met several times in public debate before their constituents. On one occasion his opponent indulged in some severe remarks upon Benton's integrity, or rather lack of integrity, and insinuated charges of a defamatory character. Benton arose, walked up to him, and after looking him fiercely in the eye for a moment, shook his fist in his face, and shouted :

"You lie, sir! You lie, sir! I cram the lie down your throat, sir!"

This occasioned the intensest feeling. Everybody expected that Benton would be shot, or stabbed at once, or at least challenged to mortal combat on the spot. But nothing of the kind occurred. His rival, it seems, hadn't any game blood in his veins. He turned pale, and attempted to go on with his speech. But the Missouri auditors turned their backs on him in disgust. They would not listen to a man who would submit to such an insult as that, and Benton had it all his own way during the remainder of the canvass.

A short time after Calhoun's death, a friend said to Benton, "I suppose, Colonel, you won't pursue Calhoun beyond the grave?" to which he replied:

"No, sir. When God Almighty lays his hand upon a man, sir, I take mine off, sir."

VI. The better side of Benton's character.

Thus far, Benton has not appeared in an amiable light. But he had his good side, and many attractive characteristics. He was honest and high toned. He was indomitably patriotic. He stood by the old flag. He had grand and chivalric ideas as to his public duty. As a Senator of the United States, his country was his only client, and he never took a fee for prosecuting a claim against her, nor lent his name or influence to help any one get into her treasury. He was a staunch friend of the poor —of poor blacks, as well as poor whites. While he was a young man, and a member of the Tennessee Legislature, he procured the passage of a bill giving the right of trial by jury to slaves. It was largely through his exertions that the public lands were thrown open to the people, that the right of pre-emption was secured to actual settlers on the public domain, and that the interests of pioneers and frontier-men were measurably protected against greedy and soulless speculators.

Benton was as true to his family and his friends as he was to his country. He could not be otherwise. Whatsoever or whomsoever he cared for, became an object of solicitude to him, and was sure of his sympathy and protection. His family affections were very strong, and his loyalty to all domestic relations was true and chivalric. An anecdote which somewhat illus-trates this phase of his character was told to me by an intimate friend of Benton's, who was a witness of the scene described. Mrs. Benton's mind became impaired by a paralytic stroke, but she always recognized her husband, and was fond of being near him. A French prince, whose name I do not remember, was visiting this country, and several distinguished residents of St. Louis becoming acquainted with him. they strongly desired to have him meet the "Great Missourian." The matter was arranged, and one evening a select party of Missourians called, with the prince, on Benton. As they were talking in the parlor, Mrs. Benton came to the door, somewhat *en déshabillé*, and stood gazing at her husband with fond and intense admiration. The attention of the company being attracted in her direction, Benton turned to see what the attraction was. On perceiving his poor wife, he immediately arose, went to her, took her tenderly by the hand, and leading her into the room with the majesty of a demi-god, said : " My dear, Prince So-and-so ; Prince, Mrs. Benton, sir." Then affectionately placing a hassock for her, by the side of his chair, he resumed his seat, and leaving one of his hands in hers for her to toy with, he went on with the conversation with that impressive dignity in which it is doubtful if he had an equal. My informant added that the prince, taking in the situation at a glance, adapted himself to the occasion with consummate tact, while all the Missourians were affected to tears.

This tough and affectionate old gladiator died in 1858. He was "Thomas H. Benton, sir," to the last gasp. He was engaged upon an abridgment of the debates in Congress from 1789 to 1856, but death cutting him short he was able to bring the work down only to the great debate on the Compromise Measures, in 1850. He finished the work by an exhibition of fortitude and endurance which was characteristic of him. Being too feeble to write, he employed an amanuensis, and carried on the work by dictation ; and finally becoming unable to speak aloud, he whispered the last few pages of the work, as the breath was slowly fading from his iron lips.

CHAPTER V.

HENRY CLAY.

I. SOME OF CLAY'S DISTINGUISHING CHARACTERISTICS.

Henry Clay was the tallest of the great Senators of his era, his height being six feet and one inch, in his stockings. He was also the most brilliant, the most chivalric, and by far the most popular. Indeed, his popularity was phenomenal—incredible to those who were not personally cognizant of it ; and he was justly entitled to every bit of it. He possessed, in remarkable fullness, all the qualities which win and retain popularity. He was kind-hearted, sympathetic, genial, tender, brave, honest, chivalric, and always true and loyal to his friends. His conscientiousness, hope, benevolence, firmness, self-esteem and love of approbation were all largely developed and active ; so that he was accommodating in friendship, but unyielding in principle ; firm but gentle ; at once proud and affable ; and both democratic and aristocratic by nature and in manner. His good-nature and his inborn American democratic-republicanism gave a familiar and hail-fellow cast to his greetings and his intercourse ; but his high-toned, chivalric dignity of character pervaded his genial familiarity, and kept his associates in mind that it was not the familiarity of a commonplace personage, but that of a high-bred gentleman who, from his own inherent graciousness and spirit of good-fellowship, chose to be thus affable.

This combination of qualities rendered Clay's address spontaneously irresistible, and the first fascinating impression was made enduring by the action of other qualities which are rightfully potential with mankind. He had a marvelous faculty for seeing everything and remembering everything—names, faces, places, events, scenes, and the topographical features of a country through which he traveled. If he met a man and spoke with him, he never forgot him or the circumstances under which they met. After spending a few hours in any place through which he passed, he could recall its features and peculiarities at any subsequent time, however remote, and remember the people he met there, and what their vocations were, to the minutest particulars. This gave him surpassing influence and popularity, inasmuch as it is pleasant to anybody to be remembered for years by a distinguished personage. The rare qualities mentioned in the preceding paragraph, which Henry Clay possessed in such affluent degree, enabled him, naturally and without effort, to make the most of these great gifts of perception and memory. Nor was it a matter of mere selfish policy for him to do so; it was the external outcome of the internal man, the spontaneous effluence of the inner spirit. He loved every part of his country

with patriotic fervor, and took an interest in
every part of it, and in all of its inhabitants,
and sympathized with them and their pursuits.
He was the great champion of American Industry, and wherever he saw a blacksmith's forge,
or a carpenter shop, or a mill, or a factory, or
a stone quarry, or a steam engine, or a printing
press, or a mart of commerce, or a farming
region, his heart thrilled with interest and
went out in patriotic affection for the people
who were at work in all those places. And
that was one of the chief reasons why he
remembered such things so well and was so
fond of talking about them. His intense,
vivid, personal and patriotic devotion to the
industrial affairs of the country, stamped his
observations of them indelibly upon his memory,
and kept his interest in them alive forever;
while his broad and generous sympathy with
working-men gave a magnetic geniality to the
interest he felt in them which was inexpressibly
attractive and winning to the toilers.

II. Leading characteristic of Clay's Mind— His Oratory.

The leading characteristic of Henry Clay's mind was penetration. His perceptive and knowing faculties were so enormously developed that nothing could escape his alert observation. He could instantaneously see clear to the bottom of any subject that came under his consideration. No sophistry could deceive him, no trick of rhetoric could mislead him, no sentimental eloquence could impose upon him. In controversy he was logical, witty, humorous, forcible, sarcastic, eloquent. His style was vehement and impassioned. His voice was full, rich, clear, sweet, musical, and as inspiring as a trumpet; it was also so penetrating that in the ordinary tones of conversation it could be heard further than the thick vocal bray of some of his rivals. When he became excited in debate, his manner was peculiarly knightly, gamy, audacious and

sometimes arrogant. As he set forth proposition after proposition with increasing energy
and fire, his tall form would seem to grow
taller and taller with every new statement, until
it reached a supernatural height ; his eyes
flashed and his hair waved wildly about his
head ; his long arms swept through the air ;
every lineament of his countenance spoke and
glowed, until the beholder might imagine that
he saw a great soul on fire and expressing
itself through an organism which spontaneously responded to its every emotion.

The effect of Clay's oratory was much
enhanced by the peculiar conformation of his
forehead and that portion of his head which lay
above it. His perceptive organs projected far
out, the crown of his head was unusually high,
and a grand curvilinear line swept from the
frontal sinus between his eyes to the apex of
his head. This peculiar conformation gave him
a commanding, eagle-like, soaring expression
which, in combination with his glowing fea-

tures, his blazing eyes and his fiery eloquence, sometimes excited the beholder's imagination until he seemed to be rising in the air with the orator. An accomplished old lady, who had known Clay from her childhood, told me that she never heard him, in one of his impassioned bursts of eloquence, without thinking of the lines descriptive of the weird magician in Coleridge's Kubla Khan :

> " And all shall cry Beware ! Beware !
> His flashing eyes, his floating hair ;
> Weave a circle round him thrice,
> And close your lips with holy dread."

The secret of this unique and resistless character must be sought in the operation of Henry Clay's environment upon his heredity or organic structure, which was exceedingly unlike that of any other human being. It has been said that he was very tall ; he was likewise very thin. Such a physical development is usually accompanied with looseness of joints, lankness of person, and general bodily awkwardness, weak-

ness and flabbiness. But Henry Clay, though
so tall and so slender, was not afflicted with
even one of those undesirable characteristics.
He was perfectly symmetrical from his crown
to his heels; his joints were firm and supple;
his frame was elastic; his bodily strength was
great; his carriage was graceful and commanding. Of course, there were reasons for this, but
it is not easy to tell what the reasons were. It
is not easy to tell just how any human organism
is built up, nor how any human being comes to
pass in his totality. It may be said that Clay's
vital force was so prodigious that, operating
with his harmonious temperaments and the
elevated spiritual nature which he possessed
from childhood, it sent his form up in graceful
contour and symmetrical development from
the sole of his feet to the crown of his head.
His limbs were long, his body was long, his
neck was long, and his head was long from the
base to the crown. And through all this singular organism the vital forces coursed in strenu-

ous, fiery currents, making Henry Clay the *livest* man of whom it is possible to conceive. It is difficult, perhaps impossible, to tell just exactly how a lily or an oak comes to pass. We know that it receives nourishment from the earth beneath, and from the sun and air above; that in a general way the earth pushes and the sun pulls, and in due time there stands the lily or the oak. We also know that Henry Clay, by virtue of his heredity and the operation of his environment upon it, had faculties which, as his development went on, took strong hold of earthly things, and other faculties which took strong hold of heavenly things; and that the earth faculties pushed and the heaven faculties pulled until there stood the phenomenal man, Harry Clay, of lofty, patriotic, genial, enthusiastic, sunny nature, who won the immeasurable admiration of millions of minds and the enduring affection of millions of hearts.

In addition to the attractive qualities already mentioned, Henry Clay was an honest man in national affairs, as well as in personal business transactions. The people believed in his honesty, and felt proud of it, and loved him more intensely because he was honest. Every one is familiar with the oft-quoted exclamation which he uttered when some of his timid friends thought that he was imperilling his chances for the Presidency. "But am I not right?" he thundered. "I'd rather be right than be President!" And he spoke the truth. He would rather have been right once than President twice. In this respect he differed from his rivals, any of whom, it is to be feared, would rather have been President once than right many times. But Henry Clay belonged to that small, inestimable class of great men who care more for the integrity of their own souls, under the all-seeing eye of God, than for any degree of worldly success and fame. Directly in line with these attractive characteristics there is, in an exordium to a celebrated speech of Clay's, which I shall by and by quote, an unconscious

revelation of a trait of his character which
greatly endeared him to his friends. In that
exordium he speaks of being "an old man—
quite an old man. But," he adds, " it will be
found that I am not too old to vindicate my
principles, to stand by my friends, and to
defend myself." There spoke the inmost heart
and nature of Henry Clay. First in his solicitude, were his principles ; second, his friends ;
third and last, himself.

Clay was industrious and economical, and
led a simple, abstemious life. He was respect-
ful and reverent towards religion. He was
beloved by his friends and believed in by the
public at large. He, of course, had enemies—
bitter enemies ; but even they did not doubt
the sincerity of his patriotism, and they
respected his genius and his probity. All these
things added greatly to the effect of his oratory.
The fact that it was Harry Clay—the chivalric,
the honest, the patriotic Harry Clay, so beloved
by his friends, and so respected by his enemies

—who was speaking, excited the imagination of the auditors and stirred them into enthusiasm. They felt sure that a great oratorical treat was coming; and when he got fairly under way in debate, and was aroused by opposition and goaded by the attacks of his adversaries, his countenance would speak as well as his tongue, and his whole body would become eloquent ; and his listeners—or at least the more emotional and less logical portion of them— captivated by the spell of his fascinating personality, would surrender their judgment and resign themselves to his will. It used to be said that Henry Clay, when pouring forth his impassioned streams of oratory, had the most *looking* countenance ever seen on mortal man. And so he had. On such an occasion, there was no passion of the soul or thought of the mind which his countenance did not mirror forth in rapid succession, as his wonderful voice expressed the same thoughts and emotions in tones which musically and vividly struck every cord of the heart. And yet his language was simple, and so was his style, and his diction flowed along in a stream of eloquence as clear as crystal, which a child could understand, and which the most experienced orator would listen to with delight.

I am fully conscious that critical readers, who are familiar with our parliamentary literature but never heard Clay speak, are ready to ask : " If Henry Clay's speeches were so very wonderful and captivating, why is it that nobody ever reads any of them now ?" The answer to that question is that Henry Clay's speeches derived their irresistible power from his irresistible personality. It was *that*--his personality which took people captive. He spoke to an audience very much as an ardent lover speaks to his sweatheart when pleading for her hand. Everybody knows that the more successful a lover's speech is on such an occasion, the less readable it is when it gets into cold print. The lover speaks for the purpose of carrying his point and winning his cause just then and there, and is content with immediate success. It was the same with Henry Clay. He spoke to win his cause right there and then and gain a favorable verdict on the spot; and no lover was ever more ardent, more vehement, more impassioned, or more successful in his appeal than Clay; and he was content with his immediate success.

Clay could tell an anecdote in a captivating way. There was a freedom, a sweep, an elegance in his anecdotal style which was very taking. One of the anecdotes he was fond of telling related to an incident which occurred in Kentucky when he was abroad, in 1814, acting as Commissioner in negotiating the treaty of Ghent. He used to tell the story for the purpose of illustrating how readily and triumphantly a Kentucky stump speaker could encounter an emergency and surmount an obstacle. Clay, while abroad, was in the habit of writing letters to his friends at home giving them an account of the progress of the negotiation of the treaty. When a letter from him arrived in Lexington, the news of its reception would be circulated, and his neighbors would assemble to hear it read. In one of his letters, which was read to an out-door crowd by a veteran politician, Clay used the phrase *sine qua non* several times. At the third repetition of the phrase, an old man, wearing a hunting shirt, who stood on the edge of the crowd, called out to the reader:

"Say, Gineral, what's siner quer non?"

The "Gineral" had no idea what the phrase meant, but he was one of the kind who are always equal to the occasion, and elevating his voice to its utmost pitch, he shouted:

"Sine qua non is an island in Passama-quoddy Bay, and Henry Clay goes for Sine qua non!"

This declaration was received with enthusiastic applause, and Henry Clay's great reputation among his neighbors as a patriotic and unflinching upholder of his country's rights against Great Britain became greater than ever.

III. CLAY'S CHIEF FAULT IN DEBATE—HIS COLLISION WITH CALHOUN.

Clay's chief fault in debate was his arrogance, and his readiness, under strong excitement, to say something so insulting that an opponent had no alternative except to challenge him, or treat him with silent disdain. A memorable instance of this kind occurred in a bitter and exciting contest which he had with Calhoun, in 1838. Calhoun had coalesced with Clay and the Whigs for several years in their opposition to what they called the despotism of President Jackson; but soon after Jackson's successor (Van Buren) began to develop his policy, Calhoun signified his intention to support the Administration in opposition to the Whigs. This annoyed Clay, because it interfered with schemes of attack upon Van

Buren's Administration, which he was maturing. Being thus annoyed, he assailed Calhoun with great acrimony, goaded him with charges of political vacillation, and taunted him with sarcastic allusions to his alleged personal tergiversations. This attack provoked the urbane South Carolinian to retort severely ; and he reminded Clay that in 1833, during the nullification contest, he (Calhoun) had over-mastered the Senator from Kentucky, and had him flat on his back. This was a legitimate and parliamentary retort on the part of Calhoun, but Clay took it as a personal affront, and when he rose to reply he was furious. Shaking his long, bony finger at Calhoun, he exclaimed. in tones of passionate resentment :

"Mr. President, *he* my master ! I would not own him for a slave !"

In those days, and in the society in which Clay and Calhoun moved, the report of a duel-ling pistol was the only voice with which such an insult could be answered ; and as Calhoun was incapable of being a duellist, a silence of years fell between those great men ; a silence which was not broken until Clay took leave of the Senate, as he supposed forever, in 1842. On that occasion he referred to his unfortunate habit of undue excitement in debate, and made such a manly and touching apology for all his offences against parliamentary decorum that there was hardly a dry eye in the Senate cham- ber ; and Calhoun, leaving his seat, walked over to Clay and extended his hand, which was cor- dially taken, and they were thenceforth friends. It must have been an impressive and affecting scene when those courtly Senatorial champions thus clasped hands after an estrangement which had lasted for years. Each was a perfect mas- ter of all the arts of courtesy and salutation, but differed sharply in spirit and manner. This difference of spirit and manner was apparent in the reception they accorded to strangers who were introduced to them. Clay, while formally polite and courteous, was so captivatingly

democratic in his hearty and sympathetic spirit
of fellowship, that a stranger, however humble
in station, at once felt at home with the affable
and cordial Kentuckian; while Calhoun,
although equally polite and courteous, was so
thoroughly aristocratic in his exquisite urbanity,
that a stranger, while charmed with his genial
and benignant greeting, yet felt that there was
a barrier between him and the stately South
Carolinian which, though slight as gossamer,
was as impenetrable as granite.

IV. THE WAY IN WHICH CALHOUN, BENTON, CLAY
AND WEBSTER GREETED STRANGERS.

The dispositions of the four great Senators—
Calhoun, Benton, Clay and Webster—were
indicated by their treatment of strangers who
were introduced to them. It was customary
for strangers in Washington to seek introductions to these distinguished men, and every
Representative in Congress was expected by
his visiting constitutents to procure them such

introductions. I witnessed many of these presentations. The usual form was: "Mr. permit me to introduce to you Mr. Jorkins, one of my constituents." I have already described Calhoun's way of responding to such introductions, and there is nothing to be added to the description.

Benton's mode of receiving a stranger thus introduced to him was overwhelmingly Bentonian. If the reader will take the trouble to recall the delineation of Benton's character, which is given in the preceding chapter, he will readily understand that Benton would consider the desire of a stranger to be introduced to *him*, an eminently proper desire. What, indeed, should anybody come to Washington for, except to be introduced to the Great Missourian? How could anybody who had come to Washington think of leaving the city without being introduced to the Great Missourian? Such was Benton's view of the subject; and Benton was the man to show the public-spirited

American citizen, who naturally wanted to be introduced to America's greatest citizen, that his patriotic aspirations were duly appreciated by the eminent personage who called them forth. So, when Jorkins, of Jorkinsville, was introduced to Benton, the Great Missourian, crushing the poor fellow's hand in his iron grip, would exclaim, with the imperious air of a demigod, and in tones that could be heard ringing through the corridors :

"How do you do, Mr. Jorkins, sir? I am very glad to see you, sir. I hope you are very well, sir. I trust you are having a pleasant visit in Washington, sir;" and so on, in a roaring avalanche of vociferous courtesy, which would fill Jorkins with trepidation, and cause him to break away as soon as possible and flee from the overwhelming presence.

Webster evidently felt such introductions to be an intolerable bore, and seldom took the trouble to conceal his annoyance. Usually, his manner, on such occasions, was freezingly indifferent. He seemed to be preoccupied and unable to bring his mind to the cognition of the rural Jorkins. Sometimes he did not even look at the person introduced, but mechanically extended his hand, and permitted the stranger to shake it, if he had the courage to do so. I have seen members of Congress turn crimson with indignation at Webster's ungracious reception of their constituents. They felt that his manner was a personal insult to them, and their constituents shared their opinion and sympathized with their indignation. Doubtless, many enemies were thus made by Webster, whose adverse influence was afterwards felt in the Whig National Conventions, of which he so repeatedly and so vainly sought a nomination to the Presidency.

I have already indicated what Clay's manner of receiving a stranger was ; but no description of it can give an adequate idea of its warmth, its graciousness, its complete satisfactoriness, both to the introducer and to the constituent

introduced.   Clay's manner to a member of
Congress who introduced a constituent to him
was such as led the stranger to imagine that
his Representative was one of the most intimate
and cherished friends that Clay had on earth ;
and his reception of the stranger caused him to
feel that for some reason it gave Clay a peculiar
personal gratification to make his acquaintance.
Then Clay would at once begin to talk with
Jorkins about affairs in Jorkinsville.   He
would remember everybody he had ever met
from Jorkinsville ; or he might have passed
through that region years before, and in that
case he would have a vivid recollection of the
country and its inhabitants.   And he would
send messages, by Jorkins, to all his "old
friends" in Jorkinsville ; and, of course, when
Jorkins got home he lost no time in delivering
the messages, in order to let his neighbors know
how intimate he had been with "Harry Clay"
while he was in Washington.   It does not
require much sagacity to perceive that Jorkins

and all his tribe, even if they were Democrats, would be personally friendly to Henry Clay.

V. Tom Marshall's Anecdote.

Thomas F. Marshall, better known as Tom Marshall, a celebrated Kentucky lawyer and orator of the past generation, (who, unfortunately, was too much given to strong drink,) used to tell how he was driven to the bottle and his law partner to the Bible, in a way which humorously but powerfully suggests Clay's marvelous ability as an advocate. "The way of it was this," Marshall used to say. "Bob Breckenridge" (Robert Jefferson Breckenridge, afterwards a distinguished clergymen)—"Bob Breckenridge and I formed a partnership when we first started out to practice law. The firm of Breckenridge and Marshall soon began to take the lead of all the law firms in Kentucky. We marched right on, without a break, until, in our own opinion at least, we were at the head of the State bar, with one solitary exception; and that

exception was Henry Clay. We had never had
a chance at him ; but we had no doubt whatever as to what the result would be if we should
have the good fortune to encounter him in open
court. We felt assured that we should at once
and forever put an end to his supremacy and
soar to the head ourselves. We watched for an
opportunity to tackle the old lion, and, after a
long wait, fortune at last favored us. We
heard that Clay had been retained to prosecute
a certain case, and we immediately rushed off
and volunteered our services to the defence, so
as to get a chance at him. Our offer was
accepted and we awaited the day of the trial
with feelings of fretful impatience solaced with
anticipations of triumph. Time dragged heavily
on, but finally the day of trial came. When it
came to the summing up, as Breckenridge and I
both wanted to take a hand in laying out Clay,
we arranged with the judge that we should
divide our time between us, and each address
the jury. I, being the junior partner, spoke

first. When I arose to begin my plea, I felt a pang of remorse at the thought that I was about to displace the splendid old man who sat before me from his proud pre-eminence, and myself take the honored position which he had so long conspicuously occupied. But I smothered my sentimentality and proceeded to business. I had made elaborate preparation for the occasion, and I did it and myself the amplest justice. I felt that Clay could hardly hold up his head after I got through with him. In fact, in my own estimation, I laid him out so cold that nothing was left for Breckenridge to do but to dance on his remains; and he did dance on them—a regular war dance. When Bob concluded and sat down, we expected that Clay would throw up the sponge without attempting any reply to our unanswerable arguments and eloquence. But not a bit of it. The old lion got up, and with one swoop of his paw he drove Brecken-ridge to the Bible and me to the bottle, and we have both been there ever since."

VI. Clay's Felicity in Exordium—A Notable Example.

Henry Clay, like Shakespeare and many another genius, was taught less by the schools than by nature and experience. He began a speech with the same masterly simplicity, directness and precision with which Shakespeare begins a drama. His exordium exhibited all the Quintilian attributes. It was brief, it was in keeping with the subject and the occasion, and it prepossessed the audience in favor of the speaker and his cause. His language and his metaphors always exactly fitted the place, the occasion, the audience and the circumstances. I will give an example which will illustrate what I mean ; but I must first venture upon a brief sketch leading up to the occasion.

When Clay retired from the Senate in 1842, it was known that he did so because, on account of the betrayal of the Whig party by John

Tyler on his accidental accession to the Presidency, Clay found *himself* in a minority in the Senate, although the Whigs had a majority there. The Tyler Whigs, following the pap spoon and uniting with the Democrats, defeated Clay's efforts to get Whig measures through Congress. As Benton graphically said, by a singular process of political filtration Clay's influence was dissipated until he found himself a dreg in the party of which for years he had been the conspicuous leader. Clay's proud spirit could not brook such humiliation, and so he resigned his seat in the Senate. And as soon as he resigned he was missed, and the masses of the Whig party began to mutter ominously. They wanted their old leader back in his rightful place. Besides, Clay was poor— poor notwithstanding his thirty-five years of public service; for he was not one of those statesmen who, on a five-thousand-dollar salary, manage to lay up two hundred and fifty thousand dollars per annum. He went home to

Lexington, (Ky.,) hired a little office and resumed the practice of the law for the purpose of earning his daily bread. Such a spectacle as that moved the heart of the nation. The rank and file of the Whig party began to clamor for Henry Clay's nomination for the Presidency in 1844. This alarmed the Democrats and Clay's personal enemies, and excited the jealousy of his rivals in his own party. It was felt by all those people that Henry Clay must be killed off; and for the purpose of killing him off a concerted system of attack was devised. Streams of detraction were poured upon him from all parts of the country; and this course was persisted in until the defamation became unendurable. In 1843 Clay announced that on a certain day he would meet his fellow-citizens face to face at Lexington, and reply to his defamers. On the day appointed, a vast concourse assembled at Lexington from the surrounding country. I hope the reader will try to summon up a mental picture of the

scene, so that he may enjoy the felicitousness
of the orator's opening sentences. There the
venerable chieftain was, in his old home, and
before him were aged men who had begun their
career in that region when he began his.
And there were the children and grandchildren
of his old comrades who all their lives had
heard eulogiums upon Henry Clay ; and there
were thousands of his fellow-citizens from near
and far who were ready to do battle for him.
And they were all Kentuckians—hunters of
Kentucky, familiar with the forest and the
chase. As the aged orator arose and stood
before them, there was the solemn hush of a
great silence. With his tall form feebly bent,
he began :

"I am an old man —quite an old man : but "
(and here he straightened himself up and his
eyes flashed) " it will be found that I am not too
old to vindicate my principles, to stand by my
friends, and to defend myself. It so happens
that I have again located myself, in the prac-

tice of my profession, in an office within a few
rods of the one which I occupied when, more
than forty years ago, I first came among you,
an orphan and a stranger, and your fathers took
me by the hand and made me what I am.   I
feel like an old stag, which has long been
coursed by the hunters and the hounds through
brakes and briars, and o'er distant plains, and
has at last returned to his ancient lair to lay
himself down and die.   And yet the vile curs
of party are barking at my heels, and the blood-
hounds of personal malignity are aiming at my
throat.   *I scorn and defy them as I ever did!*"

By this time the hearts of that great multitude were on fire, and

> " At once there rose so wild a yell,
> *   *   *   *
> As all the fiends from heaven that fell
> Had pealed the banner-cry of hell."

Cries and sobs and shouts hurtled in the air,
and there was a fierce looking around for enemies of Henry Clay ; but, fortunately, none of

his enemies were visible to the naked eye, and so nobody was lynched. But when silence and calmness were restored, the old man "rose to the occasion," and in a speech of impassioned eloquence, lasting for hours and ranging over his whole public life, he vindicated his principles, he stood by his friends, he defended himself. It was a long-continued *storm* of eloquence which rolled over the savannahs of the South and the prairies of the West, burst through the Alleghanies, swept along the Atlantic seaboard, thundered across the Middle States, broke on the granite hills of New Hampshire, reverberated through New England, and at Baltimore, in '44, gave Henry Clay the Whig nomination to the Presidency by acclamation, without the formality of a ballot.

Perhaps some of the readers of these pages remember that enthusiastic campaign of 1844, and also remember what bitter disappointment and what mourning there were when it was learned that the gallant and peerless " Harry of the West" had been beaten, as a broken-hearted Whig poet said :

> " By little Jimmy Polk of Tennessee ;
> Oolah, a-lah, oolah ee,
> Let's climb the wild persimmon tree !"

The chief cause of Clay's defeat was his opposition to the annexation of Texas and the extension of slavery. He was fighting against destiny. The annexation of Texas and all that followed in its train had to come, and fill the land with turmoil, and strife, and blood, and death, till freedom triumphed and slavery was extinguished. And so we enthusiastic admirers of Henry Clay can look back with resignation upon the omission of his election to the Presidency from the great programme of events which was prepared for us by the hand of God.

Henry Clay died at Washington, June 29, 1852, in his seventy-sixth year.

CHAPTER VI.

DANIEL WEBSTER.

I. THE GODLIKE DANIEL.—HIS GREATNESS.—HIS
PERSONAL APPEARANCE.

The last and greatest personage of whom I
have to treat is Daniel Webster. I have written of three great men—three very great men,
Calhoun, Benton and Clay; but, great as they
were, Daniel Webster, in downright intellectual
power and main strength of mentality, was
equal to all three of them taken together.

The reader is doubtless familiar with the fact
that in Webster's day he was called "The Godlike Daniel." The appellation fitted him. He
was godlike in appearance and in power. He
was not so tall as Clay, but he was much larger
and more massive in every way. He had broad
shoulders, a deep chest, and a large frame. I

have seen men taller than Webster ; I have seen men larger ; but I never saw anyone who *looked* so large and grand as he did when he was aroused in debate.

Webster's head was phenomenal in size, and beauty of outline, and grandeur of appearance. It used to be said of him that he had brain enough to make several good heads. His brow was so protuberant that his eyes, though unusually large, seemed sunken, and were likened unto "great burning lamps set deep in the mouths of caves." But large as his Perceptive organs were, his Reflectives bulged out over them. His causality was massively developed ; and his organ of comparison, which was larger even than his causality, protruded as though nature, in building Webster's head, having distributed her superabundant material as well as she could, found at the last that she had such a lot of brain matter left on hand, that, in despair, she dabbed it on in front and let it take its chance of sticking ; and it stuck. The head, the face, the whole presence of Webster, was kingly, majestic, godlike. And when one heard him speak, he found that Webster's voice was just exactly the kind of voice that such a looking man ought to have. It was deep, resonant, mellow, sweet, with a thunder roll in it which, when let out to its full power, was awe inspiring. In ordinary speech its magnificent bass notes rolled forth like the rich tones of a deep-voiced organ; but when he chose to do so, he could elevate his voice in ringing, clarion, tenor tones of thrilling power. He also had a faculty of magnifying a word into such prodigious volume and force that it would drop from his lips as a great boulder might drop through the ceiling, and jar the Senate chamber like a clap of thunder.

The color of Mr. Webster's hair, at this period of his life (1848) was a rich iron gray. His complexion was dark bronze. When he became animated, his complexion would glow so that his appearance made one think of a transparent bronze statue, brilliantly lighted from within, with the luminosity shining out through the countenance. On such occasions a singular light would play, or seem to play, upon his massive forehead, which was perhaps a reflection from the great luminous eyes that glowed with starlike splendor beneath his over- hanging brows. And from this magnificent presence there emanated an atmosphere and sense of power—of power that could be felt, of power which seized upon the imagination of the beholder, and held him breathless when he first felt it, as one stands breathless when he sudden- ly comes into the presence of a scene in nature whose sublimity is overwhelming. Nor when this first startling effect became toned down by time, did the impression of Webster's power grow any less ; as one repeatedly saw him, or became more intimate with him, the sense and conviction of his power, instead of growing less, increased ; and whenever he was aroused, and began to put forth his power, one felt that it was measureless, fathomless, endless; that there were vast floods of it still in reserve and ready to be poured forth on sufficient provocation.

II. Webster's First Appearance (of the Session) in the Senate.

I have a distinct recollection of Webster as he looked the first time I saw him. He had been ill, and several weeks elapsed, after the session of Congress began, before he came into the Senate chamber. I was occupying the reporter's seat then assigned to the members of the *Intelligencer's* corps, one forenoon, when there was a good deal of noise and bustle in the Senate, but no debate going on. Suddenly silence fell upon the chamber. I looked up and saw all eyes turned in the direction of an aisle which led from one of the doors past the reporter's seat. I looked to see what it was that so rivetted everybody's attention. It was Webster. He was coming slowly along the aisle directly towards me. I knew him, partly from pictures I had seen of him, but more from the fact that I felt it could not be anybody else, for, at the moment, I had an unreflecting, boyish feeling that there could not be two such men in the world at the same time, and that this one must be Webster. He was pale, and. walked feebly. But the picturesque majesty was there; the overpowering intellectuality was there. That enormous and beautiful head, those wonderful eyes, that stately carriage, that Jove like front, all proclaimed that the godlike Daniel had come into the Senate House and was advancing to his seat.

The silence with which Webster was received on that occasion was like the silence which his appearance in the Senate chamber, or his rising to speak, always caused. No other Senator was ever listened to with the respect which he commanded. When Benton addressed the Senate, there was more than ordinary attention accorded to him. When Calhoun spoke, he was listened to with more attention than Benton received ; Clay was still more favored than Calhoun ; but when Webster arose there was instantly a solemn hush, and the intense solicitude of great and eager expectation at once became regnant. Information that Webster was up spread like wildfire, and the Senate chamber was immediately packed with eager listeners.

Webster was in miserable health nearly the entire session, and only looked his best on a few occasions when his indignation was roused almost to rage. He sometimes had a cadaverous appearance, as though on the verge of dissolution ; he seemed absorbed and unconscious of his surroundings, and a woe-begone expression often overshadowed his lionlike countenance. But well or ill, his rising to speak was a signal for silence and concentrated attention. In "Paradise Lost," Milton, in describing the rising of a supernatural orator to address a supernatural audience, gives the only

exact description of Webster, as he looked in
those days, when he arose to address the Senate,
that I have ever met with.

> " With grave
> Aspect he rose, and in his rising seemed
> A pillar of state; deep on his front engraven
> Deliberation sat, and public care;
> And princely counsel in his face yet shone,
> Majestic, though in ruin. Sage he stood,
> With Atlantean shoulders, fit to bear
> The weight of mightiest monarchies; his look
> Drew audience and attention still as night
> Or summer's noontide air."

III. Webster's mental make-up.—His oratory.

Webster's mental make-up was, beyond all
question, the most wonderful ever known on
this continent. His perceptive faculties were
so keen, so acquisitive and so retentive that
nothing eluded their observation or escaped
from their grasp; and his analytical and
reasoning powers were so great that they could
rapidly and logically work up all the materials
which his Perceptives supplied them with. His

imagination was vivid, and his veneration was so large and active that its influence pervaded his affections and imparted an elevated and reverent quality to the operations of his mind. Thus his observing, knowing, reflecting and descriptive faculties were all powerfully developed, while his imagination and reverence gave him great richness and elevation of style. He was unrivalled in stating a case, or in describing a scene or a situation, or in developing an argument, or in telling a story or an anecdote, or in appealing to the imagination or the sympathies of intelligent people.

In order to understand Webster's greatness, we must take into consideration the important truth that the aggregation or multiplication of inferiority cannot produce superiority. It is said that the famous race horse Eclipse could run a mile in a minute. That being the fact, it would be no use to get together a score of horses that could not run a mile in less than two minutes, with the expectation of having them all together outrun Eclipse. Speed cannot be compassed by aggregating slowness. Webster's brain was so much larger than other brains, and of so much finer quality, that it developed an intellectual power which was relatively to the power of other brains what the speed of Eclipse was relatively to the speed of his rivals on the turf. It was absolutely unapproachable. A whole Senate chamberful of other and lesser minds could not successfully grapple with that one mind, any more than a whole field of less speedy horses could cope with the matchless Eclipse.

Webster had the advantage of having a body large enough to support his large brain. And then his temperaments—bilious, nervous, sanguine and lymphatic—were so completely harmonized, and his whole physical organism was so thoroughly correlated with them, that his vast brain power was perpetually nourished and kept in a vigorous state of recuperation. This gave him a wonderfully symmetrical combination of mental powers which issued in a substantialness and fineness of mind that made his intellect unrivalled for strength, endurance, warmth, susceptibility and elasticity ; for clearness, depth and breadth of view, and for acuteness of penetration and tenacity of grip. Wherefore, when Webster was thoroughly aroused, his power was irresistible. Benton had remarkable ability in building up an argument out of hard facts cemented with ingenious reasoning. Like a military engineer, he would construct fortification after fortification, and combine them so they would mutually support one another, and be impregnable against the assaults of his opponents, except when Webster assailed them. But what fortress so strong that it can withstand the earthquake's shock ? And when Webster was fully aroused, he at once plunged down to the basic principles underlying the subject, and his resistless reasoning, rising from unfathomable logical depths, with earthquake force upheaved the foundations of the strongest intellectual fortress that could be reared against him, and tumbled the whole fabric in ruins.

There was one trait of Webster's mind which seems never to have been understood; and that was its subtlety.   He was so powerful, and knew his power so well, that he almost always preferred to win his battles by sheer main strength.   But when he chose to resort to insinuating shrewdness, he could beat, at their own game, any of his opponents who relied on their subtlety for success.   Scott's anecdote of Richard Cœur de Lion's showing his strength by severing a thick bar of iron with one blow of his ponderous sword, while his Saracenic rival, Saladin, proved his skill by cutting in twain a piece of floating gossamer with his subtle blade, is often used to illustrate the mental difference of intellectual rivals.   In comparing Webster with Calhoun, it has been customary to assume that Webster is represented by Richard and Calhoun by Saladin.

There is no doubt, whatever, that Calhoun possessed a mind of almost superhuman acuteness and subtlety ; but it was not so acute nor so subtle as Webster's ; for, although, metaphorically speaking, Webster wielded the ponderous blade of Richard with unequalled strength, he also handled the subtle cimeter of Saladin with unrivalled skill.

In truth, Webster's mind was both telescopic and microscopic ; his comprehension was both vast and minute, and took in the slightest facts as well as the grandest principles. Intellectually, his reach was vast and comprehensive, his grasp strong and tenacious, his touch sensitive and delicate. His powers of delineation and elucidation were so great that he could group the details of his subject so that every fact and point and principle would stand out from the lucid depths of his argument clear as crystals, and then he could unfold and illustrate his points with captivating beauty of diction and majesty of style, investing his theme with ideal attractiveness, and pouring through it all a stream of the clearest reasoning and the soundest philosophy. His taste was severe ; he never said a word too much, nor used a word that was not suited to his purpose. When his heart was deeply moved by some great theme, and his affections were enlisted in his cause, and his intellect was ablaze with the truths he was developing, his eloquence would sometimes rise to dizzying heights and be illuminated with bursts of dazzling splendor, which were never far-fetched or incongruous, but were simply the natural luminosity of the intellectual radiance shining through the translucent gems of his thought.

Practically, Webster's mind was the perfection of common sense. No matter how wide his reasoning ranged, nor how high his imagination soared, his judgment never left its feet. His mind, like the eternal Word described by the Son of Sirach, though "it touched the heavens, yet *stood* upon the earth." His powers of abstraction and concentration were so great that, as through a mental sunglass, he could focus the burning rays of his genius upon any subject he was discussing until he set it ablaze with luminous demonstration. His power of condensation was equally great ; and his condensation never clouded .his style nor obscured his argument. Like the condensation of the diamond, it was the result of crystalliza-tion—of absolute perfection in the adjustment of parts, and the elimination from its substance of whatever would tarnish its translucency.

Quintilian, in his immortal "Institutes of Oratory," in which he lays nearly all the learn-ing and eloquence of Greece and Rome under contribution, tells us that a plea, or an oration, consists of five parts—the exordium, the state-ment of fact, proof of statement, reply to adversary, and peroration. He lays great stress upon the exordium, and says it should be brief, in keeping with the subject, and of such a nature as to prepossess the tribunal or audience in favor of the speaker and his cause. Webster was a master of exordium, as witness the exordium of his Plymouth Rock Oration, of his Oration on Laying the Corner-stone of Bunker Hill Monument, or of any of his great speeches, and especially the exordium of his speech in reply to Hayne. Quintilian considers *the statement of facts* of paramount importance, and says it must be lucid, in order that it may be easily understood ; brief, that it may be easily remembered ; credible, that it may be readily believed. (Any one who has read many of Webster's speeches must have been struck with the predominance of these qualities—lucidity, brevity and credibility—in his statement of facts. It used to be said of him that he often won his cause by his masterly statement of it, which was so clear that everybody understood it, so brief that everybody remembered it, so credible that everybody believed it.) His demonstration of his statement, his reply to his opponents, and his peroration were equally admirable, powerful and effective. Hence when he got through with a subject, there was a pretty general feeling that that was all there was of it ; that it would be useless for anybody else to say anything about it ; that Webster had been "given a mouth and wisdom which all his adversaries should not be able to gainsay nor resist." Perhaps I cannot more appropriately conclude this delineation of Webster's oratorical gifts and characteristics than by applying to him a paraphrase of what Quintilian says of Cicero, to wit : That in his grandest efforts he exhibited the energy of Demosthenes, the comprehensiveness of Plato, and the sweetness of Isocrates; and this, not by reason of any particular study of those great models, but from the felicitous exuberance of his immortal genius.)

IV. WEBSTER AS A PARLIAMENTARY LEADER.

When Webster chose to assume the attitude of a parliamentary leader in the Senate, (which he seldom did,) he played the eminent *rôle* with surpassing ability. I saw him in that part but once ; it was on an occasion which called forth all his varied powers, and especially his tact and subtlety. It was the last night of the session, and of Polk's Administration, Saturday, March 3, 1849. The session expired, by limitation, at midnight, at which hour the Thirtieth Congress completed its term and passed into history.

What was then called the Great Civil and Diplomatic Appropriation bill, without the passage of which the Government could not go on, for want of funds, still hung in the Senate, encumbered with amendments. The bill establishing the Interior Department was also still before the Senate, encumbered with amendments and bitterly opposed by a large number of Democratic Senators who could not tolerate the idea of creating a new department of the Government, with its hundreds of clerkships, just as their party was going out of power and a Whig Administration was coming in.

The Interior Department was an offshoot of

the Treasury Department, the burdens of which had become so enormous that it was necessary to relieve it of a portion of them by the creation of a new department to which they could be transferred. The bill to establish the Interior Department was drawn by Robert J. Walker, the Democratic Secretary of the Treasury, who made energetic exertions to secure its passage. But, notwithstanding Mr. Walker's influence, nearly all the Democratic Senators were strongly opposed to the bill, and a few of the Whig members took sides against it. Calhoun saw in it an insidious and dangerous attack upon State rights. He said :

"Mr. President, there is something ominous in the expression, 'The Secretary of the Interior.' This Government was made to take charge of the exterior relations of the States. And if there had been no exterior relations the Federal Government would never have existed —the exterior relations with foreign countries and the exterior relations of States with States,

and that only carried to a very limited extent.
Sir, the name 'Interior Department' itself
indicates a great change in the public mind.
What has been the cause? We are told that
the business of Government now has become
such that the existing departments are over-
loaded, and that it requires a new department
to be constituted. * * * If the departments
are overcharged, what has been the cause?
Has it not resulted from the overaction of our
Government? Is it not a strong admonition to
us to retrace many of our steps, instead of
forming new machinery to give a new impulse
to that overaction? and a very powerful
impulse this measure will give. * * * Everything upon the face of God's earth will go into
this Interior Department—Indian Affairs,
Patent Office, Land Office, Public Buildings,
all, all thrown together without the slightest
connection. This thing ought not to be. This
is a monstrous bill. It is ominous. It will
turn over the whole interior affairs of the coun-

try to this department; and it is one of the greatest steps that ever has been made in my time to absorb all the remaining powers of the States. Sir, it is time to stop. Ours is a Federal Government. The States are the constituents of the Federal Government. It is a created, and it is a supervisory power. We are, step by step, concentrating and consolidating this power, until finally we will take the last and final step, and conduct all the business under the name of the 'Department of the Interior.'"

Calhoun's remarks, of which I have given but a small portion, made a deep impression on Democratic Senators, especially Southern ones; and Webster, seeing the effect which had been produced, said:

"The argument on the other side is merely turning on a word. Why call this the Department of the Interior? The impression seems to be that we are going to carry the power of the Government further into the interior than we have ever done before. I do not so understand it. Where is the power? It is only that certain powers, heretofore exercised by certain agents, are to be exercised by other agents. That is the whole of it. And gentlemen say it is creating a new department; overshadowing everything, swallowing up State influence, and overturning all the glories of our State institutions. I see nothing of all this. I see nothing but a plain practical question. * * * There is not a particle of this bill, not a sentence, for extending the powers of the Government. It is a bill for appointing a new agent, for the exercise of already-existing powers—nothing else under heaven."

That settled the State Rights argument. The bill, however, was fiercely assailed by the opposing Democratic Senators; but Webster, powerfully assisted by Senator Davis, of Mississippi, finally triumphed over all opposition, the amendments of the Senate were receded from, and the bill was passed by a vote of 31 to 25.

Soon after the passage of the Interior Department bill, the hour of midnight struck, and it was assumed, by a number of Senators, that the session of the Senate had expired. But it was suggested that it would not do to adjourn until the Civil and Diplomatic Appropriation bill had been passed, inasmuch as the omission to pass that bill would leave the Government without funds, and compel the incoming President to call an extra session of Congress. This plea had no weight with the very scrupulous Senators who could not think of doing anything so unparliamentary as to proceed with legislation after the Thirtieth Congress had, as they alleged, expired. Benton, Cass, Calhoun, and several other Senators, sat silent in their seats. It was understood that they were of the opinion that the session of the Senate had terminated at midnight. Here was certainly a very grave question, and Senators did not seem to know what to do about it. At last Webster arose. All eyes were fixed on

him. He spoke briefly. After a few explana-
tory words, he said : '' I am of opinion that
the session of this House, which commenced on
this third day of March, until we vote upon the
Appropriation bills, must continue without
regard to C-L-O-C K-S !'' The word clocks filled
the Senate Chamber with articulate thunder,
every reverberation of which expressed the
utmost scorn of the idea that the session of the
Senate had come to an end. It seemed as
though Webster had smashed the horologe of
Time, and that clocks should be no more. That
one word, as hurled forth by Webster, seemed
to settle the question ; but he added a few
sentences to give Senators sufficient reasons for
holding that the Senate was still in lawful session, and would be in lawful session until it
should of its own motion adjourn.

A few minutes afterwards a message was
received from the House of Representatives,
which threatened to defeat the passage of the
Civil and Diplomatic Appropriation bill, to

which a portentous amendment. providing a government for the Territories of New Mexico and California, had been proposed by Senator Walker, of Wisconsin, on February 20th. Senator Bell, of Tennessee, offered a voluminous amendment to Mr. Walker's amendment. Webster proposed another amendment as a substitute for both Walker's and Bell's ; and Senator Dayton, of New Jersey, offered still another amendment modifying Webster's. The attempt to engraft a bill for the government of Territories upon an appropriation bill was looked upon by many Senators as unprecedented and unparliamentary, and it led to prolonged debates. The Appropriation bill was finally sent back to the House of Representatives, where it originated, with several dozen amendments, including what was called the California amendment (the one providing a government for Territories), which was No. 53 on the list. The message received after midnight from the House of Representatives announced that said House had concurred

in the 53rd amendment of the Senate, *with an
amendment* (of their own) *to that 53rd amendment*, in which they asked the concurrence of
the Senate ; and that they had receded from
their disagreement to the other amendments of
the Senate.

This action of the House of Representatives
opened the door to an endless debate. Their
amendment to the Senate's amendment was
obnoxious to Southern Senators, some of whom
thought they saw a lurking Wilmot Proviso in
it. Other Senators objected *in toto* to the
foisting of a territorial bill upon an appropriation bill, while others revived the question of
the incompetency of the Senate to legislate
after the hour of midnight. Others offered
additional amendments to the existing amendments, so that an amendment to an amendment
to an amendment to an amendment, running
back like "The House that Jack Built," was
before the Senate, with other motions piled on
top of motions. In the midst of the turmoil,

Senator Yulee, of Florida, made a motion to adjourn *sine die*, but nobody paid any attention to it, and the confusion increased. Senator Turney, of Tennessee, who seemed to be in great mental and moral distress, solemnly requested that the Secretary of the Senate should be directed to note the hour upon the journal. This caused a lull, while every Senator looked at his watch, or at the Senate clock. It was then 20 minutes past 2 o'clock A. M. I will now copy a few lines from the record.

MR. WEBSTER. What is the question?

PRESIDING OFFICER. The question is upon the motion to adjourn *sine die*.

MR. WEBSTER. I protest against it. We have no right to adjourn without the consent of the other House.

A SENATOR. The President of the United States has gone home.*

MR. WEBSTER. Very well, if he chooses to go; but we shall have the pleasure of sending him a bill between this and 10 o'clock to-mor-

* It was customary for a President, when there was a session of Congress on the last night of his term, to occupy a committee room in the Capitol, where bills, as they were passed, could be brought to him for his signature; and President Polk had been in attendance, in accordance with that custom.

row morning.   I protest against it for the sake
of the republic.

This was an effectual notice by Webster that
he was going to hold on till the Appropriation
bill was passed, and the notice was emphasized
by the decision of the Presiding Officer that
Webster's point against adjournment was well
taken, and that the Senate could not adjourn
sine die without the consent of the House of
Representatives.   This point having been set at
rest, the debate on the Appropriation bill proceeded. As the discussion went on, Senators got
excited, called one another names in a parliamentary way, and became savage in attack and
venomous in retort.

Sometimes the confusion was so great that
speakers could not be heard, and it was impossible for the reporters to follow the line of
debate through the overwhelming turmoil.
Senator Foote, of Mississippi, boisterously insisted
that the session had terminated at midnight;
that Senators whose term of office expired on

the third of March were no longer members of
the Senate and had no right to take part in the
proceedings ; that, in fact, the assemblage was
not a senate, but a public assembly, a town-
meeting, that was legislating without a shadow
of authority. He became so intolerably weari-
some and offensive that at last he was hissed.
This only caused him to talk still more volubly,
and finally groans were heard. "I know my
rights, and will maintain them, too," exclaimed
Senator Foote, "in spite of all the groans that
may come from any quarter. Groans will have
no effect on me," he magniloquently declared,
"even though they shall equal the thunders of
the most terrific volcano that ever shook the
eternal mountains." And on he talked, with
tantalising verbosity.

When things had got at their worst, and
everybody was utterly weary of the arid turmoil,
Webster arose, and ignoring all the folly and ill-
temper which had been exhibited, he stated the
legislative situation and pointed out the precise

work to be done in order to accomplish what
ought to be accomplished before the Senate
adjourned.   His statement exhibited all the
Quintilian characteristics—lucidity, brevity and
credibility—in the highest degree.   And there
was a matter-of-course air pervading it, a lofty
and courteous taking it for granted that every
member of the Senate agreed with him, which
was irresistibly attractive and persuasive.   That
power of his, of which I have spoken, manifested itself by drawing the minds of Senators
in the wake of his mind as a vast and powerfully propelled steamer draws floating objects in
its wake.   A parliamentary calm followed his
remarks, and a sensible and dignified discussion
of the questions at issue was begun.

I never saw, on any other occasion, such
power, such tact, such wisdom, such wit, such
humor, such dialectic skill, such profound
knowledge of human nature, such all-embracing
common sense as Webster displayed that night,
or rather, that morning.   He was opposed by

some of the ablest and most adroit debaters in the Senate, and by several of the most ignorant and stupid ones. The able debaters he drove out of the field with the heavy artillery of his logic ; the adroit ones be tripped up with superior dialectic skill, and left them lying helpless ; the vain and ignorant ones be soothed into quiescence with consummate tact and laid them away in beds of downy flattery to self-conceited repose ; the pretentious and contentious ones he either crushed by downright logical force, or else persuasively coërced them into silence by elegant sarcasm. He took interruptions with imperturbable patience, with but one exception. Senator Foote repeatedly asked permission of him, on different occasions, "to be allowed just to make a few remarks in explanation," etc., and Webster goodnaturedly gave way. But at last, when the discussion was hinging on a critical point, and Webster was speaking with great conciseness and power, Foote jumped up and said, " Will the Senator from Massachusetts allow me

to state "—" If the Senator will be brief," inter-
posed Webster. " For God's sake be brief," he
added, with a volume of voice and a thunder
roar which swept Foote out of the debate so
effectually that he didn't get back into it for
nearly an hour.

The Senate repeatedly got into what seemed
inextricable parliamentary tangles, with motions piled on motions and amendments upon
amendments. In every such case Webster
would disengage the tangles with inexhaustible
patience and the most cheerful good humor. In
short, the magnificent old chieftain was so
good-natured, so witty, so humorous, so vast
and comprehensive, so terse and lucid, so high-
toned and majestic that he constantly inspired
not only good-will and friendliness, but
admiration and awe, and finally gained an all-
commanding influence over the Senate. As
the hours passed on, his opponents gave up
point after point; the Senate's amendment to
the Appropriation bill was receded from, the

bill was passed, and the Senate adjourned at 7 o'clock on Sunday morning.

I recently read that entire debate, as it stands defectively reported in the *Congressional Globe*, and felt a keen regret on realizing how impossible it is for people, who have only the printed record of such memorable scenes, to get anything approaching to an adequate idea of their true character. If the sun were removed from our solar system, and it were possible for mankind to survive its removal, and years afterwards people who never saw the sun should read an account of what our system was before the sun was removed, they would get just about as vivid a notion of the truth as a person who never saw Webster in animated, vehement debate would get in reading a report of that Senatorial scene, in which he was the central orb, from which emanated so much of its light and warmth and power and glory.

V. Other Characteristics—Webster's Incomputable Service to the Country.

It is acknowledged by every one who is acquainted with the facts that Webster was as preëminent in intellectual power as I have represented him; that Horace Greeley spoke the truth when he said : '' Webster's intellect is the greatest emanation from the Almighty Mind now embodied." It is also acknowledged that Webster was somewhat lacking in character. It is, of course, understood that character does not come from intellect, but from morality, virtue, benevolence, courage, conscientiousness, firmness, fortitude. A man may have a transcendent intellect, and yet be a coward, a liar, a thief, a scoundrel of the most despicable kind—

"The wisest, brightest, meanest of mankind,"

as Pope wrote of Lord Bacon. Webster's firmness, self-esteem and conscientiousness were comparatively weak ; and this organic defect was sometimes manifested in moral obtuseness and infirmity of purpose. For this reason, Webster never was and never could be a popular party leader like Clay. In an intellectual contest, no human being could contend successfully with Webster ; but when the intellectual contest was ended, and the victory won, he would lapse into indifference and suffer the fruits of his victory to be snatched from him by men of inferior intellect. Perhaps it was fortunate that his nature was thus defective ; because, if, in addition to his vast and matchless intellect, he had had the imperious character and indomitable will of Clay or Benton, he might have become an intolerable dictator in public affairs, and been too powerful and predominant for his country's good. In a government "of the people, by the people, for the people," the people must govern themselves, and there is no room anywhere for a dictator.

The majority of the people of the United

States little know how much they are indebted to Daniel Webster. He did for us a work which, in its way, was as necessary and valuable as the work done for us by Washington was in its way. He taught the country what the true nature of its government is. He logically, powerfully, clearly and popularly demonstrated the baneful character of the disunion and secession heresy, which, started by Quincy, was afterwards so destructively wrought out by Calhoun. If it had not been for Webster, Calhoun would have carried everything before him ; there was nobody else who could cope successfully with the brilliant South Carolina dialectician, or with his equally brilliant coadjutor, Hayne. And if the country had become convinced that the alleged right of secession was in very truth and fact a constitutional right, and that any State might constitutionally secede from the Union when it imagined itself to have a sufficient provocation for doing so, what would have been the inevitable result ?

The result would have been that the people
would not have fought to maintain the Union,
and we should now be dissevered, discordant
and belligerent, instead of united, fraternal and
prosperous, sweeping on to a destiny of incon-
ceivable grandeur. But Webster, having won
the battle for the Union in the Senate, the
people were ready to win, and did win the
battles for the Union in the field :

> " Nor is it aught but just,
> That he, who in debate of truth hath won,
> Should win in arms, in both disputes alike
> Victor."

VI. AN OCCASION WHEN WEBSTER WAS ENRAGED.

In the ordinary course of legislation, Webster did not speak often. It was only when
some important topic was before the Senate
that he condescended to mingle in the debate.
On one occasion he was thoroughly aroused,
and electrified the Senate with a terrific burst
of indignation. It was when a side issue on

slavery was under discussion, and the debate was so irritating that nearly every one who took part in it lost his temper. Butler, of South Carolina, (Calhoun's colleague,) became very angry and indulged in a fierce and vituperative attack on what he called the bad faith of the North. He accused the Northern States of breaking every compromise ever entered into between them and the South as soon as they could see a chance to make money by breaking a compromise. He declared that this bad faith had been exhibited so often on the part of the North, that he had become sick of the word compromise ; or, as he put it, smiting himself, as he spoke, upon his bosom : "I am sick at h-e a-r-r-r-t of the word compromise."

When Senator Butler sat down, Webster was seen to be getting up. I use that form of expression, because the getting up of Daniel Webster was not a mere act ; it was a process. The reader may have seen an elephant get up, and may have been impressed with the magnitude

and evolutionary character of the operation.
Webster's getting up was vastly more impressive, because it was intellectualized, moralized,
spiritualized. The beholder saw the most
wonderful head that his vision ever rested on
rising slowly in the air ; he saw a lionlike countenance, with great, deep-set, luminous eyes,
gazing at him with solemn majesty ; in short,
he saw the godlike Daniel getting on his feet,
and his heart thrilled at the thought of what
might be coming.

On the occasion to which I refer, as soon as
Webster arose, information of the fact was
circulated all through the Capitol. " Webster's
up, and he's mad," was the smothered cry which
sounded through the corridors and ante-cham-
bers. That was sufficient to excite the liveliest
interest. The Senate chamber was immediately
filled by an eagerly expectant audience. After
Webster got upon his feet, he slowly rocked
himself back and forth for a few moments, with
his head bowed and his hands clasped behind

him. Then he looked up, and around, and fixed his gaze upon Butler.

> " His look
> Drew audience and attention still as night
> Or summer's noontide air."

The suspense was intolerable. Every heart stood still. Slowly unclasping his hands, and letting them fall by his side, and speaking in low, deep, musical, metallic tones, surcharged with intensity and power, Webster said :

" Mr. President, the honorable member from South Carolina, who has just taken his seat, says that he is prepared to say boldly that the Northern States have not observed, but have broken the compromises of the Constitution."

MR. BUTLER (in his seat). " I said it."

MR. WEBSTER. " Yes, Mr. President, he said it. It is no duty of mine to take up a glove that is thrown to all the world ; it is no duty of mine to accept a general challenge. But if the honorable member shall see fit to be so obliging as to inform the Senate, in my hearing, on what occasion the State, whose representative I stand here, has forborne to observe or has broken the compromises of the Constitution, *he will find in me a* COMBATANT *on that question.*"

Senator Mangum, of North Carolina, subsequently said that the word "combatant" weighed at least forty tons ; and as it fell from Webster's lips, he took a step towards Butler, his bronze complexion glowing as with inward fire, his brow clothed with thunder, his eyes blazing lightning, both arms raised, and his huge form towering in all its majesty. It is impossible to give a description of the scene which will convey any idea of the effect which Webster produced. I will only say that whoever did not see Daniel Webster on that occasion (or has not seen an equivalent spectacle) cannot have any conception of what a magnificent human being God's creative hand can fashion.

Butler moved uneasily in his seat, muttered

"I'll answer the gentleman; I'll answer the gentleman," and attempted to rise. But he was restrained by his friends (Calhoun among others) who were near him. They did not wish to provoke Webster into making one of his over-whelming speeches, in favor of Massachusetts and the North, at that time. They foresaw the great parliamentary struggle which was coming on, and under the lure of the Presidency in 1852, they were trying to keep Webster from assuming a pronounced attitude of antagonism to their wishes. So Calhoun, with an air of childlike innocence, entered into the debate, and with consummate adroitness turned it into a cold, passionless discussion of constitutional points. Webster was appeased, missed a great opportunity, went on his way under the lead of the subtle influences which enveloped him, made his famous seventh of March speech in the following year (1850) in favor of the Com-promise Measures, and having been thus used for their purposes by the South and its Northern

allies, he was contemptuously cast aside by them
in 1852, and died in October of that year;
going down to his grave under a heart-crushing
load of disappointed ambition and political
despair.

VII. Source of his Political Despair.—His
Passionate Love of the Union.—His
Incomparable Political Insight
and Foresight.

Webster's political despair was caused by the
vision of future events which his vast powers of
comprehension and his keen and far-reaching
insight revealed to him. He saw clearly into
the governing principles of things, and he saw
clear to the bottom. He never mistook effects
for causes. He never got lost amid the chaotic
antagonisms of phenomena, but always struck
right back to the fountain heads whence the
streams of events flow. In his Plymouth Rock
Oration (1820), he indicated the dangers with
which the country would ultimately be threat-

ened on account of slavery, and the undue growth of monopolies of wealth and power. The anti-monopolists of the present day go to that oration for their best ammunition, and you see what Daniel Webster then said on the subject (sixty-nine years ago) now printed in large type in anti-monopolist newspapers.

I have said that Webster's veneration was so large and active that its influence pervaded his affections and imparted an elevated and reverent quality to the operations of his mind. It in fact pervaded all of his mental and moral attributes, and was perceptible in whatever he said. There was a subtle element of reverence in his wit and humor, which gave them an indescribable charm and power. Every one who is familiar with his eloquence knows that it is marked by a Hebraic, Biblical quality which sometimes imparts to it unusual solemnity and grandeur. So controlling was veneration in Webster's character, I have no doubt that when he did anything wicked he did it reverently.

Upon his patriotism, the effect of his reverence was strongly marked. He reverenced the Revolutionary Fathers, of whom his own revered and beloved father was one; he reverenced their motives and their principles; he reverenced their patience and their fortitude; he reverenced their trials and their sufferings; he reverenced their wisdom and their virtues; he reverenced their achievements and their moderation in the day of their success; and, above all, he reverenced the American Union, which was the net product to the country and to the human race of all their long and sometimes hopeless struggle.

Webster not only reverenced and loved the Union with all his heart, mind, soul and strength, but he understood its significance, its worth, its necessity, its immeasurable importance to its own citizens and to mankind. Wherefore, Webster's patriotism was not only rooted in the deepest, widest, clearest logical perceptions which it is possible for a human mind to have on any subject, but it also had the overruling force of a religious passion ; and his love of country, dominating all his views of public policy, bound his conscience in invincible devotion to the Union and to its preservation at all hazards and against all contingencies. To him, slavery, or any incident or phenomenon connected with the legislation or institutions of the country, was infinitely of no consequence in comparison with the preservation of the Union. Only preserve the Union, and time and the ultimate patriotism and good sense of the people would take care of everything else. Abraham Lincoln was animated by a similar love for the Union and guided by similar broad views as to the conditions of its preservation, when, in reply to Horace Greeley's open letter, addressed to him in August, 1862, he said :

"My paramount object is to save the Union, and not either to save or destroy slavery. If I could save the Union without freeing any slave, I would do it ; if I could save it by free-

· ing all the slaves, I would do it ; and if I could do it by freeing some and leaving others alone, I would also do that."

It is vain for persons who do not understand these attributes of Webster's mind, and these traits of his character, to attempt to sit in judgment upon his political course. As well might purblind ducklings presume to sit in judgment upon an eagle's flight.

Webster's wonderful power of analytical vision, rendered prescient by his deep, intense, elevating reverence, enabled him to see that the compromise measures of 1850 would have but temporary influence ; that the conflict between slavery and freedom could not be permanently pacificated ; that war between the North and the South was inevitable ; and the patriotic old demigod, who loved his country with the very religion of patriotism, was glad to take leave of the scenes in which he had so long been, as Benton said, " the colossal figure, bearing the constitutional ark of his country's safety upon his Atlantean shoulders."

Events have justified Webster, and shown how mistaken were the hordes of abolitionists who howled upon his track in 1850. I say this with all the more freedom because I was one of the fiercest of the howlers ; and I will add that my howls were honest ones. We were all as conscientious as we were mistaken, and it has all turned out for the best, because God can make as effectual use of fools as of sages. Webster spoke in 1850 with the events of 1861 before his vivid intellectual vision. And when the crisis which he foretold came, and the events which he foresaw in 1850 began to take place in 1861, Seward, Chase and other alarmed anti-slavery statesmen then voted in Congress for measures which Webster was hounded to his grave for advocating in 1850.

In the last paragraph of his renowned speech in reply to Hayne (1830), when speaking of the then threatened dissolution of the Union,

Webster said : " While the Union lasts, we have high, exciting, gratifying prospects spread out before us, for us and our children. Beyond that, I seek not to penetrate the veil. God grant, that in my day at least, that curtain may not rise. God grant, that on my vision never may be opened what lies beyond." His prayer was granted. He did not live to see the sectional and fraternal strife which he alone of all the men of his time clearly foresaw and was absolutely sure would come, unless the people of the whole country would learn, and abide by, and carry out in all their political relations, the great truth taught by Goethe—

" Only *the law* can to us Freedom give."

And happily, when—to paraphrase his own touching and eloquent words from that same speech in reply to Hayne—his eyes were turned for the last time to behold the sun in heaven, their last feeble and lingering glance beheld the gorgeous ensign of the Republic, known and

honored throughout the earth, still full high
advanced, its arms and trophies streaming in
their original lustre, not a stripe erased or pol-
luted, nor a single star obscured. And thanks
be to God, owing largely to the workings of
Divine Providence through the mighty mind
and the great, patriotic heart of Daniel Webster,
the gorgeous ensign of the Republic, with many
bright stars added to its ample folds, now floats
more proudly than it floated when Webster's
eyes closed upon it, and it floats over a Union
whose enduring cohesion' has come forth tri-
umphant from the severest test to which any
nation or government could be subjected.

I have scarcely hinted at the faults of the
four conspicuously great men about whom I
have written in this little book. Of course

they had faults, and I intended to refer to them, for the purpose of pointing sundry morals. But I find that I have not the heart to do it. They have gone forward into their eternal environments, "every one unto his own place." It matters not to them what commotion we may raise around their memories here; but it does matter to us; for, with what judgment we judge we shall surely be judged. Those great men passed their lives in the service of their country. They worked for us long and well, every one according to his own light. The unfortunate political aberration which overtook him I loved best, can now be forgiven. They were sincere, honest, great-minded, large-hearted patriots, and looked for their reward to the increasing honor and glory of their country, and not to her spoils or her plunder. While we remember their services with gratitude, we can look forgivingly upon their errors. And so, to the accomplished Christian gentleman Calhoun, to the tough old iron-clad Benton, to the eloquent and chivalric Clay and to the godlike Daniel, BENEDICTION AND FAREWELL.

FINIS.

INDEX.

[303]

314   INDEX.

END.

WHAT LEADING NEWSPAPERS SAY ABOUT

THE NEW YORK LEDGER.

———◆•◆———

[FROM THE NEW YORK MAIL AND EXPRESS.]

Under the energetic and capable management of Mr. Bonner's Sons, his great family paper, the New York *Ledger*, is making long strides forward; and brilliant as its past has been, the future bids fair to surpass it. Mr. Bonner was indeed fortunate, not only in founding a great and beneficent literary enterprise, but in leaving descendents who are fully capable of carrying out successfully even larger plans than the founder proposed.

[FROM THE PHILADELPHIA LEDGER.]

The New York *Ledger* has successfully maintained its popularity in despite of that rivalry which its own great merits provoked. Instead of a mere story paper, the *Ledger* is so broadened as to make it a chronicle of the most sentient thought of the time ; it educates as well as entertains. It is none the less a story paper, and its stories are good stories ; neither is it any the less a paper which readers of the widest culture may read with profit and pleasure.

[FROM THE BOSTON EVENING JOURNAL.]

Robert Bonner's Sons are determined to bear the mantle which has fallen on their shoulders beyond any mark yet reached. As a popular story paper, the *Ledger* has made its chief reputation, but it has much enhanced this by enlisting in its service the pens of men whose words have touched the varied keys of the human heart.

[FROM THE BROOKLYN STANDARD UNION.]

Robert Bonner's Sons have taken hold of the *Ledger* with an energy that is refreshing. The father worked eighteen hours a day to establish his publication ; the sons are working night and day to make a success that will eclipse all their father's efforts; they have started in the right way; first, they are determined to keep up the *Ledger's* standard of purity, and, second, they are determined to employ the brightest pens to be found in the fields of wholesome literature at home and abroad.

[FROM THE CLEVELAND PLAINDEALER.]

The contributors to the *Ledger* include the most notable writers in the field of history, science, biography, poetry, literature, and all that relates to the educational interests and the social and domestic well-being of the people. The *Ledger* is suited to the wants of all, old and young, and is distinctively the family literary paper of the country.

[FROM THE ALBANY EXPRESS.]

Among the illustrated weekly papers, none has reached and maintained a higher standard of uniform excellence than the New York *Ledger*. The *Ledger* is firmly fixed in the confidence and the affections of the American people.

[FROM THE NEW YORK SUN.]

This week's issue of that interesting and entertaining family paper, the New York *Ledger*, has been issued under a new form, and presents a very pleasing appearance. There are several new features to the paper. The *Ledger* in a new dress will naturally be a surprise, but the improvement is so marked that the surprise is very satisfactory.

[FROM THE PITTSBURG POST.]

The New York *Ledger* has never had a rival in its special field, and the enterprise and sagacity with which it is now conducted indicates that it does not in the future intend to invite one or put up with one.

[FROM THE PHILADELPHIA EVENING CALL.]

The New York *Ledger* has ever been, in the best sense of the name, a " Family Paper." It has been a welcome visitor in the best homes of the land. Never an impure word nor a suggestion that was not ennobling has appeared in its columns; clergymen and historians, as well as novelists and poets, have been its constant contributors. Robert Bonner's Sons are proving themselves worthy of their father, which is saying much, and there can be no doubt that their success will be greater.

[FROM THE JERSEY CITY JOURNAL.]

Robert Bonner's Sons have taken hold of the *Ledger* like old journalists, and are following the excellent example set by their father. The *Ledger* has always been a clean, pure family paper, and has employed the best talent in the world. Mr. Bonner's sons propose to keep up this policy, and every lover of pure literature must wish them success.

[FROM THE SHERMAN (TEX.) COURIER.]

The New York *Ledger* is the greatest of story papers.

[FROM THE NEW YORK STAR.]

A new era is marked in Robert Bonner's Sons success, the New York *Ledger*. A few weeks past its patrons were more than pleased with the announcement that Mrs. Frances Hodgson Burnett, at an enormous expense, had been engaged to supply the *Ledger* with a serial. Close on to this announcement its publishers give its readers a delightful surprise by an issue this week having little of the appearance of its former issues. The mechanical features are most important, for therein lies the great change.

[FROM THE HARTFORD (CT.) TIMES.]

The New York *Ledger* of this week will be a surprise to its readers. The improvements add vastly to the results of what we have always regarded as the best, cleanest and most wholesome family story paper in the country.

[FROM THE NORRISTOWN (PA.) WEEKLY HERALD.]

The New York *Ledger* has always been the handsomest and best of the family story papers, and it is now more so than ever.

www.ingramcontent.com/pod-product-compliance
Lightning Source LLC
Chambersburg PA
CBHW021217270326
41929CB00010B/1167